I Painted the Light

I Painted the Light

Using Spirituality to Heal from Childhood Sexual Abuse

Jeanne Grimes

BALBOA
PRESS
A DIVISION OF HAY HOUSE

Copyright © 2013 Jeanne Grimes.

All rights reserved. No part of this book may be used or reproduced by any means, graphic, electronic, or mechanical, including photocopying, recording, taping or by any information storage retrieval system without the written permission of the publisher except in the case of brief quotations embodied in critical articles and reviews.

Balboa Press books may be ordered through booksellers or by contacting:

Balboa Press
A Division of Hay House
1663 Liberty Drive
Bloomington, IN 47403
www.balboapress.com
1-(877) 407-4847

Because of the dynamic nature of the Internet, any web addresses or links contained in this book may have changed since publication and may no longer be valid. The views expressed in this work are solely those of the author and do not necessarily reflect the views of the publisher, and the publisher hereby disclaims any responsibility for them.

The author of this book does not dispense medical advice or prescribe the use of any technique as a form of treatment for physical, emotional, or medical problems without the advice of a physician, either directly or indirectly. The intent of the author is only to offer information of a general nature to help you in your quest for emotional and spiritual well-being. In the event you use any of the information in this book for yourself, which is your constitutional right, the author and the publisher assume no responsibility for your actions.

Any people depicted in stock imagery provided by Thinkstock are models, and such images are being used for illustrative purposes only.
Certain stock imagery © Thinkstock.

Printed in the United States of America.

ISBN: 978-1-4525-6998-7 (sc)
ISBN: 978-1-4525-7000-6 (hc)
ISBN: 978-1-4525-6999-4 (e)

Library of Congress Control Number: 2013905504

Balboa Press rev. date: 04/30/2013

Contents

Preface . . . . *ix*

Part I: Introduction
Introduction 3

Part II: My Life
Growing Up 13
The Façade is Cracking 31
The Nightmares 37
Counseling 41

Part III: The Sacred Heart
The Sacred Heart 55
Healing the Mind 63
Healing the Body 83
Healing the Spirit 115

Part IV: The Unity Principles
Principles of the Unity Church 129
First Unity Principle 135
Second Unity Principle 139
Third Unity Principle 145

Fourth Unity Principle 159
Fifth Unity Principle 169
Summary of Unity Principles 175

Part V: Forgiveness

Three Levels of Forgiveness 187
First Level of Forgiveness 189
The Second Level of Forgiveness. 197
The Third Level of Forgiveness 203

Part VI: Summary

Summary 217

Part VII: Afterword

Afterword: My Father's Death 223
About the Author 237
Appendix Music List. 239
Bibliography. 243

PREFACE

In 1986, I was a successful math teacher in my early thirties. I was living in a cute apartment, happily divorced and dating handsome men. I enjoyed laughing with my friends and dancing the night away on the weekends. I had a large extended family and I treasured our holiday gatherings.

So why did I want to kill myself?

Why was I counting pills and thinking of clean and pain-free ways of ending my life. What was this heavy underlying sadness that would invade my world at times and bring me down hard? I would often ask myself, *What's wrong with me? What is this darkness in me that feels so horrible and heavy? What is so bad that I want to kill myself?*

One day I was driving to my parent's home. I was feeling incredibly hopeless and sad. I saw a huge, dump truck coming from the opposite direction. *That's it,* I thought. *I could end the suffering now and make it look like an accident. It'll be quick and painless.* So I swerved my car into the oncoming lane in front of the dump truck, bracing myself for the impact.

But then I looked up at the truck in front of me and into the driver's eyes. I saw his shocked face and his look of terror. I instantly realized that I may kill him too and bring sadness to his family. I quickly jerked my car back into my own lane.

What is wrong with me? I asked myself again. This incident scared me enough to seek out professional help. I found a therapist and together we began searching for the root cause of my depression and my desire to end my life. I knew my childhood was a mix of love and abuse. There were wonderful camping vacations and family gatherings, along with physical, mental and emotional abuse. But nothing appeared to be so bad that it would create thoughts of suicide.

Slowly, my kind therapist helped me unearth a forgotten past filled with sexual abuse. Hundreds of repressed memories surfaced of my father sexually abusing me from infancy throughout grade school, and into my teens. Some memories came exploding out while others slowly let me peek at the event in short glimpses. Thankfully, my personal counselor and a wonderful support group of sexual abuse survivors helped me through this time.

And I healed. Slowly, I healed.

The years of therapy helped me with the severe depression and the utter chaos caused by the new found memories, but I still felt empty inside. The Pandora's Box that I had opened brought lots of negative feelings. I felt small and unsure. I felt fragile and insignificant. There were times that I hated myself and felt inadequate. I felt unequal to everyone else. The inner child was very scared. She felt very tiny. What could I do to make this child feel safe and sure? How could I make myself better? How could I make myself feel really healed? Where were the answers to feeling whole? How could I do this? I wanted to fully recover from the abuse. There had to be a way to fully heal and be whole.

Counseling helped me in so many ways. I learned to set healthy boundaries, became aware of my inner dialogue and established new ways of being. But nothing in my therapy sessions made me feel completely whole. Nothing in the self-help books helped me get rid of the lingering pain and sorrow. Nothing at church helped me to deal with the deep feelings of shame and unworthiness. How could I piece together all the fragments of me to create a whole and healthy person? How could I feel confident and self assured? Where were the paths to find my way to the answers?

I started reaching out to different practices like meditation, music and yoga. I came to find that the power to heal myself was within me. The power was WITHIN ME to heal. Not outside me, not from a book or from a therapist, but within me. Through a deep spiritual journey I found the true me hidden inside and allowed the sacred feminine to awaken and expand. The journey was long and hard and utilized methods not typically found within most clinical counseling settings. But my healing journey has made me whole, happy and at peace. I had to undo many teachings and learn new ways of thinking and doing and feeling and relating. I had to explore my inner spirituality on many levels. Many changes were to take place. Great changes! Wonderful changes! Painful changes! But it is all worth it. To feel at peace inside is a wonderful feeling that I wish for all of you. My goal is to share these ideas on how I combined the mind, body, and spirit into one cohesive unit and found peace within. You have peace within you too. We all do.

It has taken me over six years to write this book. The process has been both painful and enlightening as I've captured my feelings and memories on paper. I avoided it for months on end, until I had the courage to revisit and relive the emotional events of my life. This was not written like a novel from beginning to end, but in bits and spurts, as ideas would surface.

I've organized this book into three sections. Part One will give you some background information about me, my childhood, the abuse and my individual and group counseling. My hope here is to let you see into my life, so there is a distinct before and after impression of me. I hope to share how traditional counseling, coupled with spirituality, can lead to quicker, more in-depth healing.

Part Two focuses on The Sacred Heart. The Sacred Heart has mind, body and spirit elements, and I'll describe how specific spiritual practices can help you heal these components from the abuse. I'll describe how specific spiritual practices can help you further heal from the abuse. I'll share my own stories, tell you about my recovery and share recommendations for creating your own action plan to a more peace-filled life.

The principles aspired by the Unity Church are explained in Part Three. They were very helpful in my recovery and I believe the spiritual messages within each principle will help other victims of sexual abuse.

Part Four deals with the huge topic of forgiveness and Part Five is a summary of the lessons I've learned during my healing process.

While reading about my journey, take what resonates with you and leave the rest behind. Some practices may feel comfortable to implement now and some you may want to do later on down the road. Some of the ideas you may never feel like practicing, and that's okay. This path may not be for everyone. If my book helps one person feel better about themself and allows him or her to live a fuller life, then the time spent writing this is worth it.

To all the counselors in the world, I offer this short note. You have a caring heart and a genuine desire to help others or you wouldn't be in this profession. I invite you to consider incorporating some of the ideas in my book into your sessions with your clients, both individually and in groups. It must be frustrating to see your clients hit roadblocks in their recovery process. Allow the creative muses to enter your healing space and watch your clients blossom. Allow the left and right parts of their brains work together to repair the neurological, emotional and psychological damage that has been done to your clients. Please consider reading Gary Zukav's wonderful book, *The Seat of the Soul*. You may find his material on spiritual psychology helpful.

To those who teach counseling courses in our colleges and universities, explore the idea of adding these concepts to your curriculum. It is your duty to equip these budding counselors with the tools that will make them most effective in their practices. I encourage you to seek out research, beyond what I have listed in the Appendix, of the beneficial effects of alternative therapies when added to the standard cognitive approaches. My ultimate goal would be to change the way we counsel patients. Allow the models of therapy to expand to include the spiritual aspects of a person. By helping to heal the entire mind, body and spirit of a sex abuse survivor, you'll make significant strides in returning that wounded soul into a fully-functioning, happy individual.

I ask you to read about my healing journey with an open mind. Let's start the wonderful journey to wholeness!

Thank you,
Jeanne Grimes

PART I: INTRODUCTION

"I Painted the Light" at the age of 5

Introduction

"I Painted the Light" at the age of 5

I LOVED KINDERGARTEN! I LOVED PLAYING with other children my age. I loved all the play stations where we could explore so many different toys and make-believe worlds. I enjoyed the teachers and their wonderful enthusiasm. I was free to learn and experience so many new things. It was the first time I had ever been read a book and the fairy tales were fun and fascinating. The stories had wonderful messages and colorful, imaginative pictures. I just loved kindergarten! My Appalachian culture at home was so dull and dreary compared to this bright engaging environment. I finally had something other than my sheltered existence at home.

I also learned about finger painting. I was allowed to use a huge piece of paper from a flip chart—all my own! What a privilege to have a page nearly as big as me to use all for myself! I couldn't wait until it was my turn to paint! I loved dipping my little fingers into the gushy paints. I loved smooshing the paint between my little palms and feeling it squish between my fingers as I clasped my hands together and squeezed. The slurpy sound and the slippery wetness were delightful sensations. Kindergarten was the beginning of my own personal expression of self.

On my day to paint, I donned my Dad's huge old denim workshirt as my painting smock. I dipped my hands into the yellow paint jar and began smearing the wonderful color on the page. I went back for more. And more. And more. I ignored the vibrant reds, the colorful greens, the rich blues and purples. All I wanted was the bright yellow. And on and on I dipped my hands into the yellow paint jar and covered the entire page. Not one corner of my huge paper canvas was left untouched by my little yellow hands.

My teacher asked if I wanted to use the other colors or add some accents to my page. "No," I told my teacher. I shook my head adamantly back and forth. I thought to myself, *This is all I want. This wonderful, beautiful, luminous yellow!* On and on I painted, covering every speck of white space with that radiant, shimmering yellow. And when I was done, I stood back with all the confidence of a self-assured five year old and I beamed at what I had created.

There it was! I had recreated my yellow space! I had painted the Light! My warm, safe light. I was so proud! *Wait til I show this to Daddy!* I said proudly to myself. I was oblivious to the curious looks of my teachers.

The paper hung on the draped line to dry. It must have taken much longer to dry than the other children's paintings because there was so much paint on that paper. Other kids had painted a crude rendoring of their house, or maybe their Mom and Dad and the family dog. Others had created a modern art design with swishes of blue and a blot of red or a hand print in green. But no one had entirely covered their whole canvas with paint. And certainly no one had used only one color. My painting was so different than the others and yet I didn't care. The excitement I felt was exhilarating! I was so thrilled about my yellow space! The anticipation of taking this beautiful creation home to my Dad was overwhelming.

At the end of the day, my wonderful canvas was released from the metal clips holding it up to dry, then rolled carefully into a tube-like shape. A trusty rubber band was placed around its belly and then the masterpiece was placed in my now clean little hands. *Oh, wait til I show Daddy!* the little voice in my head screamed. *Wait til I show him this!*

My morning kindergarten class was over and Peggy, an older neighbor girl, walked me home. My excitement was spilling over the top and I wanted to run the five blocks home, but Peggy would have none of that. We took our usual pace and it felt like an eternity. When I got home, Mom had lunch waiting for me and asked about the papers I had brought home. She looked at my painting and must have mumbled something about it, but I didn't care if she even looked at it. I really didn't care what she thought about it. This wasn't for her. It was for me and Daddy.

My Dad worked day-shift at a local factory and would get home about four o'clock every day. He would come in the side door of the house, climb the four steps from the landing to the kitchen, sit down in his chair at the kitchen table and take his work boots off. That day, I stood in the kitchen bursting with anticipation, eyes wide with excitement, my grand painting held tightly in a roll in my little hands. But I had to wait until the work boots came off before I could show him anything or talk to him about the events of the day. That's just the way it was done. I watched as the long shoe laces of the work boots were unthreaded from the hooks along the top of the boot. Then the laces were loosened from the eyes along the front of the boot, and finally the boot was pulled off. First one—thud! Then the other—thud!

By now, I'm jumping up and down, squealing with delight as I waited for him to finish. Now I finally got to show him what I made! I unrolled my painting. It was quite an effort for my little tiny hands to hold both the top and bottom of the paper, stretching as far as I could, nearly covering myself with that large canvas. "There, Daddy, see?" I exclaimed.

But after my gleaming yellow masterpiece was unveiled, he gruffly growled, "What the hell is that?"

I couldn't believe my ears! He doesn't know what this is? My little brain raced with confusion! I looked at my painting. I looked at him. What?! What do you mean, "What's that?" He should be absolutely thrilled with my creation. He doesn't even know what it is. I stared at him with puzzlement. I felt confused but still expected him to recognize, at any time, the beautiful, warm, peaceful place that we had experienced together many times. That glowing light that envelops me and takes me away when he comes to my bed and touches me.

"Well, what is it?" he yelled.

"Daddy!" I said. "This is where I go when you do those things to me!"

Bam! His large dirty hand immediately took a full swing and slapped my tiny face, knocking me down. I laid on the linoleum floor in disbelief as he screamed at me, "Don't you EVER talk about that again!"

Stunned, I stare at him with my mouth open. I can't believe what is happening. This is a good thing I've done. I've painted the Light! Why is he so angry? Why am I being punished? He continued to scream and lunged at me. I continue to cry. I'm confused and terrified as he rips up my painting and continues to hit me. What is going on?

My confusion and shock are overwhelming. I had expected high praise from him for painting that lovely place that I thought we both experienced when he came to my bed. Little did I know that I was the only one who experienced the Light during those times. So instead of my painting being admired, I was being beaten and my work of art was being torn to shreds. His loud and angry voice was terrifying me with threats of further harm if I ever spoke of this again.

I had painted my yellow God, my yellow safe place, the warmth of the deity, the safe surrounding of love and light, of peace and unity, of warmth and safety. I loved the sensation of floating amid the yellow light of joy, of unlimited joy, the safety of God, of Spirit, of oneness. A place of no pain, no cares, no anguish, no limits, no harshness, no frustration, no mental pain, no physical pain, no emotional pain.

This is where I belong! Among the Lights. Among Spirit. Amidst the Love. The unending, undivided, undimensional Love. A place where I could float effortlessly among the other spirits, the other Lights, and be one with God.

Here I would escape the confusion of the abuse. Why is this happening? Why don't you love me? Why don't you take care of me? Instead you hurt me! You feast on me! You take away my innocence! All for your own depravity. I'm so little. I'm so tiny. I'm so weak. Why? Why? Why? Why? I don't understand! I don't know why this is happening!

The evil look in his eye scares me so. His greed! His need to take from me! I don't understand what is happening to my little body—the harshness of this brutal attack, the fear, the torture, the pain, the confusion! The evil laugh he would laugh as he delighted in my body was so other-worldly. I would shudder when I heard this laugh. I knew it was to be a very bad time when he laughed like this. The sinister, evil sound was enough to send me into a feeling of shock. I knew from this guttural sound that his behavior would be brutal and would last a very long time. I would somehow distance myself from the situation and almost become a robot, obeying his commands with a detached expression. It was no use to fight anymore. I knew I could not win. I just gave in and checked out. I became a mere machine who was separate from my spirit, my soul. I would detach and let him have my body while I drifted away safely.

I experienced such lightness as I lifted out of my body. I would slowly drift up and float to the corner of my bedroom ceiling. I'd look down on the two of us lying on the bed. I'd then turn to the Light and drift off towards it. I could look back and see what was happening, but I did not feel what was happening. I was disconnected from by body and no longer felt the pain and fear. I had numerous out-of-body experiences long before I ever knew what they were.

My angels are waiting. Here they are! Again! "Oh, Hello! You're here!" I say to them. They're little angels, little cherubs, just like me! They're playmates, smiling and happy to see me. They're giggling and playful. They take my hands on either side and off I go with them to the Light. We play and rotate. I sing and dance and float with them, and with all the other angel Lights. We're weightless and free! I rotate and spin within my own orb of Light. It's like swimming in Light! We fly in any direction. We fly within the Joy! I'm safe here. I'm happy here! I'm free!

As I'm writing about this memory, I'm being strongly reminded by Spirit that this is who I really am. I am the Light. My purpose, my guides say, is to tell you that: *You are the Light! You are not your body and your experiences don't define you. You are the Light!*

Sometime later, I would awaken from a deep sleep feeling disoriented and groggy. Confusion filled my little head as I wondered what had happened and what was wrong. A feeling of being disconnected from the world—like I was walking among the world, only more like floating, looking at the objects around me with an objective air—in the world, but not of it. I felt spacey, light-headed, and distant. I wouldn't be fully back in my body at times. I wouldn't remember the abusive intrusion to my psyche or the ravage attack on my body. I would be dreamy, feeling insecure and in need of comfort. A warm hug from either my Mom or Dad would do, just someone to welcome me back to this world. Sometimes I would get it, but many times not. I would need to find my own comfort by sucking my thumb and wrapping myself in my blanket until I finally re-entered my body fully and felt "normal." Whatever that is! The feeling of separateness left me feeling a void, an emptiness inside.

And so when I was five, I painted the Light. I painted that happy place where I flew with the angels and the other Light beings. I painted the serenity the best that I could. I painted the Love and the Joy on a single piece of flip chart paper for my Dad to see. And now for the world to see. Everyone in the world needs to see who they really are—Lights! Bright, joyous Lights!

My spirit went away to a beautiful yellow Light that was safe and warm and peaceful during the abuse. And even as I write this, I don't really know where I went. There are several theories and guesses that sound plausible, but I don't really know the mystery of what I experienced. Did I rise beyond physical reality and go inside to the soul and rest in the glow of my inner light? Did I have guardian angels or spirit guides who whisked me off to some other level of existence to escape the horror of what was happening? Did I have an out-of-body experience where I escaped into another realm and saw the light that so many who have a Near Death Experience talk about? Or is all physical reality truly just a dream or illusion, and during these times of nightmarish events, did I really just awaken to the Truth of my being, to my inner Light, to escape the ugly dream?

Of course, I never talked about the painting or the Light again to anyone. The whole experience was repressed for the next 25 years. The memory of my painting surfaced while I was still involved in group therapy. I told my therapist and the group participants about this memory, but I just received a lot of raised eyebrows and blank expressions. No one had an idea or an explanation for my out-of-body experience. There were no suggestions that I may want to explore metaphysics and the importance of the Light in spiritual texts and teachings. It wasn't until many years later when I learned about Near Death Experiences, the inner Light and the importance of the Light within metaphysical realms that I began to put my personal childhood experiences into a spiritual context. Did my escape into the Light allow me to heal quicker than others who had been sexually abused? Did it allow my spirit to escape the deeper, more serious emotional damage that comes from sexual abuse that I had seen in my group therapy settings? Was I somehow special in that I was given an alternate reality or escorted to a safe haven during the abuse and the others were not? Or did we all have this Light experience at one time or another and I was lucky enough to remember it?

What does it all mean? I don't know yet. But I am so glad to know with all my heart that another reality or realm of existence does truly exist. I know because I've been there. And I'm not afraid to go back to the Light that I painted that day.

Part II:
My Life

Growing Up

I AM A COAL MINER'S DAUGHTER. I was born in the Appalachian Mountains south of Pittsburgh, PA on April 12, 1954. My parents, John Wesley Grimes and Marion June McNutt, grew up in the coal mining community around Uniontown, PA. They married on June 3, 1947 and rented my mother's childhood home in Uniontown for seven years. My parents wanted to build a home of their own and the usual custom for the area was to build it in stages as money allowed. So they bought a piece of land, dug a hole and built the basement. They put the flooring down for the first floor, but instead of building the rest of the house, they put roofing material on the floor and we lived in the basement, which my mother always referred to as the "foundation." Their plan was that when enough money was saved, the rest of the house would be built. I don't remember the foundation, I was too small, but I have seen pictures of me in it. The basement was separated into rooms using curtains as room dividers. We lived there for about 2 years.

Dad and Me, 19 mos old, 1955.

The coal mining industry was in decline and eventually the coal mine closed and my father lost his job. He, along with many other men from the area, had to look for jobs elsewhere, even outside of Pennsylvania. He found a job in Cleveland, OH and worked there for awhile. He stayed in Cleveland during the week and traveled back to Uniontown on the weekends. He then found another job in Canton, OH, about 60 miles south of Cleveland. My parents sold the foundation home and moved to Canton. We rented an upstairs apartment on Louisiana Ave very close to the Stark County fairgrounds. It was a nice neighborhood with two-story homes crowded together on narrow lots. It had a big front porch that the first floor tenants used. Our garage was located in the back and was accessed by an alley that ran behind the homes. We played in the small backyard and in the alley behind the house. My folks really missed their family and nearly every weekend we would drive back to Uniontown on Friday after Dad got off work. We would stay with either set of grandparents or other aunts and uncles for the weekend and then return back home on Sunday evening. My brother, Mark, was born while we lived in that apartment.

I remember playing in the alley out back. I thought it was so cool to be able to run in a street! Well, it wasn't actually a street, it was a large path with two gravel ruts in it. But to me, it was a street, and it seemed to go on forever (a whole block, at least!) and I could run! After being cramped up in a small apartment, it felt good to have the freedom to run. We also had an outside staircase that we climbed to get to our apartment. In the winters, it seemed very cold with the wind whipping around us on the open stairs. The landing at the top was high. It always felt scary on that landing, looking down at the ground, waiting for Mom or Dad to unlock the door.

For Easter one year, Mark and I got baby chicks—nice, soft yellow live baby chicks. They were adorable and we kept them in a cardboard box under the kitchen sink. Our sink did not have a full cabinet underneath with doors but rather a curtain that would slide across to hide the pipes and the contents stored underneath. Well, the chicks grew and grew and eventually we had a full size hen and a giant rooster under the sink! That rooster would start to crow in the mornings and wake everybody up. Both of them started pecking us really hard, as chickens will do. So my Dad had to get rid of the hen and rooster. They certainly were not appropriate indoor pets in a small second floor apartment! I don't know what he did with them, but I do remember that rooster sticking his head out from beneath the sink through the two curtain panels and looking at me. It was nearly as tall as I was. I sure was scared of that thing!

When I was about 4, my parents purchased the house where they still live to this day. Located in the northeast side of Canton, it is a big two-story house with two extra lots, one on each side, a big front porch and a detached two car garage. They were able to buy the house with the help of the owner. He financed the home in some way that allowed them to move into a home bigger than they really could afford at the time. I remember the day we moved into that house. I was standing on the sidewalk leading up to the front door and staring up amazed at this huge house.

Mom found out she was pregnant with my youngest brother, John, around the time of moving into this house. I'm not sure if she found out before or after we actually moved in, but they have shared stories with me about how they were stressed about having another mouth to feed and the costs of having another baby. They were already stretched to the max on their budget with this new house, so having another child certainly caused them some anxiety. In order to help with the house payments, my parents rented out the second floor as a separate apartment to tenants. There was only one front entrance into our home so for quite awhile, the renters would have to come through our front door, enter into our living room, and then take the stairs up to their place. There wasn't much privacy for either family, but it seemed to work. Upstairs, one bedroom was converted into a small kitchen and another bedroom was used as a living room. That left one bath and one bedroom upstairs. Sometime later on, Dad cut out a new entry door at the bottom of the stairs onto the front porch, so that the tenants could enter their apartment privately from the front porch. He sealed off the staircase from our living room to make it a private entrance.

The first floor was plenty big enough to house our family. We had a kitchen, an eat-in dining area, and a big living room. On the back of the house, an addition had been built before we bought the place. It included a long hallway that led to a bathroom, a big hall closet, and an additional bedroom, which became my parents' room. The house's original dining room had been walled off from the living room and kitchen and was now only accessible from that back hallway. That former dining room became the bedroom for all three of us kids. The boys slept in a double bed and I had my own single bed in that one big bedroom. There was a large window in our bedroom with a big window seat in front of it. I have sweet memories of writing plays and creating talent shows with my brothers and cousins and performing them for the adults. We would use that window seat as a stage for our performances.

John, Mark and Jeanne, 1961.

Our home was filled with such a mixture of stress and happiness. I felt loved by my mother with all her attention and care. She was generous with her hugs and would constantly tell us she loved us. Mom always had meals cooked for us and clean clothes to wear. She would help with homework and school projects as much as she could and took an interest in our studies. She loved helping us with Halloween costumes and was quite ingenious when it came to creating homemade outfits. They were usually way better than store bought costumes and I would be the envy of the neighborhood girls. I especially remember being Cat Woman complete with ears, a long tail, long black fingernails and a black outfit. Mom was still a kid at heart. She loved being with her kids, but almost too much so. She never really developed her own sense of self, never really had friends, and would often ask me to stay home from elementary school to play with her. I would look at her with amazement that a parent would actually ask their child to miss school. But I was too much of an achiever and perfectionist to miss school. I would remark that I had a test that day or I was afraid of missing something and she would respond that I could make it up the next day.

Other children may have really taken advantage of this situation, but I loved school and didn't want to miss. She didn't like being alone so much. She had no close friends that I know of. She would talk to the neighbor ladies, but I don't remember her really having her own friends, her own life, her own activities outside of the home. She was expected to be there when we got home from school and then when Dad got home from work. Later on, she started working at the local A&P grocery store as a cashier to help the family with extra spending money, but she mainly worked nights and weekends. So, during the day she was by herself, cooking, cleaning, ironing—the typical duties of the American housewife of the fifties and sixties. She expected me to help with these duties also. I didn't mind helping out, but the resentment started building when my brothers were old enough to help and I was told that they didn't do certain jobs because they were considered "women's work." I really did not understand why a boy or man could not clean a toilet or scrub a floor. I rebelled against the idea that because they had a penis they would never have to clean the bathroom tub. Mom bought into the traditional roles of the female and I questioned them—quite vocally at times—all to be shut down by either my mother, or eventually my father, if I pushed the idea.

I hated the subservient feel of cleaning floors on my knees knowing that if I were a boy, I would never be expected to do it. To this day, I still resist cleaning the bathroom or scrubbing the kitchen floor. I still hear the phrase that it is "women's work" and cringe. Cleaning a floor has nothing to do with male or female and has everything to do with creating a clean and welcoming environment in my home. Even though I know all this, the 'little me' still throws an internal tantrum when the idea of cleaning the kitchen floor enters my mind. These old teachings and internal conversations stay with us so long and can control our emotional equilibrium if we're not careful. To me, scrubbing the kitchen floor on my hands and knees was the lowest form of servitude forced upon me. A man could not lower himself to clean a floor on his knees. He was above that!

Let's heal our feminine energies. Take the one activity or comment that stirs the angry crone in you and let her roar. Let her vent the injustices put upon women throughout history. Write it down, type it out, scream it in your car, beat that rug (or tennis racket or drum!). Let out that primal energy in a safe and private way. We don't need to yell at anyone in particular. It's not about them. It's about us. It's about releasing the angry torrent caused by our submission, by our lack of choices, by our barred entrance into the realms of men. It may be a big thing, or a little thing like cleaning my kitchen floor, but by releasing this steam, we will enter into a more quiet place. We have to let loose the hot vapors swirling around inside us and allow the peaceful indwelling Spirit to come to live there in tranquility and serenity. Give up the anger in yourself and you give it up for Mother Earth as well. You give up the anger for all of humanity, both masculine and feminine. There was a time to be angry. The anger served us well in creating change, but now it is lodged inside us, even when it's not necessary any more. My husband, Wayne, will gladly swab a brush around a toilet bowl. So why do I still feel resentment about the roles my parents played in their traditional society? I'm not expected to succumb to these out-dated modes of conduct and yet I still carry that little spark of indignation around inside me. That internal voice of "How dare you expect me to …" still lingers and creates unrest within me. And for what? That was many, many years ago. It's time to let go of the righteous anger and be peaceful now. I'm thankful for the awareness of this anger so that I can continue to work on it and not let it control my emotional state. Will this anger leave eventually? I hope so, but for now I'm just amused at the inner workings of myself and thank God for my Swiffer.

I have many happy memories of growing up in my family. We used to go camping many weekends in the spring, summer and fall. The place we would visit most was Berlin Reservoir, about 35 miles northeast of Canton. We would also go to Atwood Lake, Tappan Lake, Salt Fork Reservoir, the Ohio River and smaller private campgrounds in the local area. Along with these weekend trips, our family would always take a long vacation each summer in a different part of the country. We would camp in wonderful places in the woods, along streams, by the ocean, in the mountains or in the desert. I've been in just about every one of the 48 contiguous states because of these family vacations and I am very thankful for that. Camping was good for me in so many ways. Playing in nature is always fun and therapeutic. But I also learned how big and wonderful the world was outside of my sheltered world in Canton, OH. And maybe more importantly, there was the element of feeling safe from my father's advances while we were camping. There was little room for privacy and hidden activities when you have 5 people staying under one temporary roof. So I knew on our camping weekends or on longer vacations, I was usually safe from his prying hands and cruel intrusions.

We camped in a tent for many years and then eventually bought a pop-up camper. We also had a boat that we would take with us for water-skiing. I had lots of fun during those trips. I would be free of a lot of the responsibilities of watching my brothers and cleaning house, so I could be free to play and explore nature. I could just be a kid. I learned to catch frogs and crayfish in the streams, bait my own hook and fish with a bobber, which I always called a 'bobbin,' like the spool of thread inside a sewing machine. I could take a fish off its hook and could even wrestle a big catfish, if I caught one, although they were uglier and slimier that the other fish. I got used to seeing snakes and other woodsy critters in the wild.

My folks loved the Rocky Mountains and we took many trips to the west. When we were going on a long trip, they would pack the trailer and make the back of the station wagon into a bed for us three kids. We would leave on Friday evening after Dad got off work, and he would drive all night while we kids slept in the back. We would wake up the next morning somewhere in the corn fields of the Iowa and by that night we would set up camp looking at the mountains of Colorado. That was a smart way to travel with little kids. Fewer bathroom stops and fewer squabbles. We would then have the next two weeks to make a large circle throughout several states as we visited Old Faithful, or Four Corners, or Grand Canyon, or Pikes Peak, or Mount Rushmore or Crater Lake. We went to rodeos and old mining towns and often saw large animals out in the wild. We experienced the delight of bears walking up to our car in Yellowstone National Park. We once spotted a giant, wild elk with a full rack in a clearing in the woods. We stopped and walked into the clearing and stood within 10-15 feet of this majestic animal. Another time, while traveling along a flat expanse of land we saw a herd of wild buffalo off in the distance. We stopped alongside the highway, viewed them through our binoculars and watched the entire herd eventually cross over the road right in front of us. We learned later from park rangers that all of these activities were very dangerous and that any of the animals could very likely have charged us at any moment without notice or provocation. Ah well, sometimes the ignorant (or stupid!) get lucky! These were magical moments as a child. To watch large wild animals up close in their natural elements was awe inspiring. It's much different than in a zoo or wildlife preserve setting. To be out in nature and see the beauty of wildlife within its own environment is truly spectacular!

We often camped with my Aunt Shirley and Uncle John on the weekend trips and even made some long excursions with them as well. They eventually had five children in all, but when there were only 2 kids in their family, we once took a trip with them to California… in one station wagon. That's four adults and 5 children packed into one car! We pulled a utility trailer that held our two tents, the dining canopy, suitcases, food, stove and lanterns. We would pack a cooler on our big 'driving' days with lunch meat and bread inside and eat in the car while we traveled down the road. We had this clever contraption made with aluminum bars that slipped over the front bench seat. There were two trays that folded down, one in the front and one in the back that acted as our tables. The women would usually be in the back seat making sandwiches, while the guys were up front driving and navigating. I'm sure it saved them a lot of money with nine mouths to feed, and we made good time by not stopping for lunch. At times other than lunch, the space between the two men up front was reserved for the kid who was the crankiest or the one misbehaving the most. The same was true for the space between the Moms in the back seat. So the best seat in the house, so to speak, was the third seat in the station wagon. This seat faced backwards which was always a fun place to ride. We would make faces at the folks traveling behind us, play travel games like Punch Bug, license plate count and I Spy. We were also the farthest distance possible from any parent. I often would be sitting in that seat, unless I got carsick, which I did quite a bit, or when I couldn't stand the antics of all my younger travel companions. I was the eldest of the five kids, 3 boys and 2 girls, so sometimes I just couldn't stand to be back in that third seat with two little ornery boys!

Mark, Jeanne and John, 1966.

On our weekend camping trips at Berlin Lake, we would often camp with Aunt Shirley and Uncle John, his sister and family, plus some older cousins on my Dad's side who were married and had young children. We often had 3 motor boats to use during a weekend and I was always out in one of the boats. I learned to water ski at about 11-12 years old. Since I was such a skinny little kid, I had trouble putting on the heavy skis and couldn't hold the water skis upright by myself before takeoff. So, one of the adults would stand in about chest-deep water along the shore and hold onto me by the sides of the life jacket. They would hold me until I could get my skis on and then hold them parallel and upright in the water. Someone in the boat would throw me the tow rope and I'd hold onto the handle while they slowly took out the slack. Once the rope was taut, it was almost like being suspended in air. The grown-up behind me was holding me back by the life jacket, while the tow rope was slightly pulling me ahead. Someone, either me or the adult with me, would yell "OK!" and off the boat would go! I looked pretty funny in those early years with bony sticks for legs and a skinny body. It didn't take much of a wave to knock me down, but I loved the water and practiced whenever I could. I was always skiing or being the watcher, and later learned to drive the boat and pull the other skiers. I soon learned to slalom which was really much more fun than two skis. I helped teach my younger brothers and cousins, and even other adults to ski. I never tired of being on the water and that, I'm sure, influenced me to eventually buy a home on a lake. The soothing effect of water, coupled with the wonderful wildlife that populates a lake, makes it a wonderful place to live. I now enjoy a kayak, canoe and pontoon on my lake. The noisy power engines and high energy activities have been replaced with soothing quiet rides atop the aqueous world.

One night when I was about ten years old, the two Dads took us night fishing! We climbed down some rocky ledge to a shoreline by the lake. It was so cool to have the lanterns lit and be casting our lines into the dark abyss. I'm sure the Dads never wet a line that night, what with taking care of all our rods and reels and worms and wiggling bluegills! This night stands out for two reasons. One, it was just so cool to be out walking in the dark with lanterns and fishing in the dark with our Dads. It was just the right amount of scariness to be exciting! Secondly, I almost went up in flames that night! I wasn't fishing too long that night before something big hit my line and took off with my bait in its mouth. My little Zebco reel screamed! I screamed! My pole bent way over and then pulled to one side. Dad coached me through the process of bringing in my huge catch as I continued to scream. I eventually brought in a large carp that was probably 14-16 inches long. At my age it looked like Moby Dick. I was so excited! I couldn't wait to tell everyone back at camp about my big catch. And instead of waiting until the whole fishing group was ready to leave the shore, I wanted to go back and tell my Mom and Aunt Shirley and all of my older cousins and their wives right then and there. So, I took off running back up the rocky ledge, down the campground lane to our campsite. As I'm running toward our campsite where everyone was sitting around the campfire, I'm screaming, "Mom! Mom! I caught a fish! I caught a big fish!" And just as I neared the campfire, I tripped over a tree root and went flying directly into the fire! My chest landed right on the wood branches in the flames! My older cousin saw me flying through the air and came out of his lawn chair, just in time to pick me up out of the flames. It was almost like he caught me in air and continued my flight and swooped me down on the other side of the campfire! I never got hurt, never had a scratch or a burn, and best yet, I never quit talking! When he set me down on my feet, I was still exclaiming how big this fish was and how it pulled from left to right and on and on and on! The whole crowd of 10-12 people just burst out laughing at me! I stopped talking and looked at them wide-eyed. "Why are you laughing at me?" I asked. "You just fell in the fire and you never shut up! You just kept talking!" they answered. "So what," I exclaimed, "you've got to see this fish I caught!" Well, that story and my ability to talk through anything followed with me for a long time!

During my childhood there were tickling episodes that caused me great stress. During family gatherings, my aunt would hold me down on the floor and tickle my sides and belly. The tickling would start out innocent enough, but when I had had enough, I would start yelling "Stop it!" or "Noooo!" At that point the tickling would increase as she dug her fingers into my skin even harder, to make sure I couldn't get away. Her playful nature would turn into something sinister and disturbing. My squirming, wiggling attempts to sit up and run were met with a stronger hold to keep me captive.

She would start saying demeaning things to me like, "Oh, you baby! Can't you take it?" or "No way, you're not getting away from me!" I would start yelling for help from my Mom or Dad, or any of the relatives who were in the room, but instead of helping me, they laughed and encouraged my aunt.

Worse yet, they would completely ignore what was happening to me and pretend I wasn't even in the room screaming for their help. The tickling would continue until the pain on my skin was simply unbearable and I would start to cry. I would look up at the couch and try to catch someone's eye, but they wouldn't even look at me. I would be screaming and bending my head back looking up over my forehead to see if someone, anyone, was noticing my pain. It was like I couldn't stand being in my skin and was trying to wiggle out of it and away from the feelings.

As soon as I started crying, the verbal abuse increased into belittling name calling and attacks on my personality. My family members would say things like "What's wrong with you? Can't you take a little kidding?" "You big baby!" "What are you so upset about? She's just playing with you?" There was no sense of urgency from any of the adults that I was a child in pain, being abused and needing their help! There was almost a sense of them all uniting in their denial that there was anything wrong or abnormal going on in the room at all. My crying would increase and my pleas for help would turn into pitiful wails of "Nooooooo!" all while my aunt was laughing and ridiculing me and continually tickling me.

I would eventually start sobbing so hard that I couldn't catch my breath. My body would go into uncontrollable spasms as I tried to somehow endure the pain. I would start having hiccups in between the sobs as my little lungs were gasping for air. The tickling would go on for what seemed to be forever and not one person came to my aid.

Finally, she would release me and make a big production of letting me go. "There, you big baby! Go! I don't know what you're crying about! Go on. Get out of here! What's wrong with you?! I was just having fun with you. You know I didn't mean to hurt you!" The other family members would be laughing at me and making fun of my sobs and hiccups. They would continue spitting their rude comments at me as I ran off to find a quiet place in the house. I would continue to sob and gasp and hiccup in some remote corner until slowly I would catch my breath. Gradually, the body-wrenching sobs and hiccups would ease. It took a long time before my breathing would resume a natural pace again and my heart would settle into its normal rhythm. I would somehow try to regain my composure so that I could face the family again. I knew I had to be strong because they would start teasing me again as soon as I resurfaced into the family area.

My nerves were shattered.

Again.

My body was violated.

Again.

The fear awakened.

Again.

And this time I was humiliated in front of people.

And I was ignored.

Again.

This happened many times over my childhood, as a toddler, as a small child and even as old as a nine or ten year old girl. I was abused by a family member, humiliated and shamed in front of family members, and then ignored by these family members. What the hell was wrong with them? What made them think this was funny? Why didn't anyone take care of me when I was crying for help? Was I invisible? Did I just exist for their sick enjoyment?

What possible pleasure did my aunt get when she made me cry? Why did she continue to tickle me until I started sobbing and have hiccups? How could the adults in the room sit and watch a child be tortured and not do something? My aunt had one type of sickness in her, some need for control - a sick need to have power and command over someone. The other family members had a different kind of sickness - a need to see their female child, especially a bright and strong first-born, be debased to a weak, limp and sobbing mess of flesh. This sadistic behavior happened occasionally to the other children in the family, but it was really centered on me.

How do I forgive my aunt?

How do I forgive this sick family?

How do I let go of the anger, the shame and the feelings of helplessness?

How do I process the feelings of being a nobody, invisible and not worth helping? These were the folks who supposedly loved me. They said they did. But it didn't feel loving to be here at all.

And then it would be safe for awhile. They would act sort of normal and caring for awhile. And my guard would go down and I'd start to trust them again. I would be cautious when the extended family got together at our home. I'd stay away from my aunt's reach for awhile. But then she would snatch me and it would start all over again. The unpredictability was what made home life so difficult. The element of surprise caught me off guard and unprepared for the attacks. I would trust and let my guard down and then I would be grabbed again. It made me doubt my ability to read people and situations. I stopped trusting my inner voice and my gut feelings. It wasn't until much later as an adult that I started paying attention to the inner voice again and trusting my intuition.

How do I trust anyone to touch me? How do I know if they mean to caress or control? What does it really mean when someone says they love you? Is anyone authentic? How do I know if there is anyone that can be trusted?

One of the positive aspects of my childhood came from helping my Dad navigate on family vacations. My Mom was terrible with directions and had no sense of north, south, east and west. She literally got lost one day driving home from work one day. When I was in elementary school, she was a cashier at the A & P grocery store which was about a mile and half away. She traveled that one road to our house several times a week, but one day she got behind the plaza where the store was located and couldn't find her way out of the neighborhood she was in. But she could see the main road. So, she just drove over the lawns and made her way back to the main road and found her way home! So, needless to say, she didn't do much driving and certainly no navigating on our trips. At a very early age, I learned how to read road maps, determine where we were on a highway and give accurate directions using the atlas, travel brochures, and campground books. We didn't use the 'TripTiks' that were available from AAA then and there wasn't the Internet, MapQuest or GPS services like we use today. I either had or developed a good sense of direction from all this experience and could decipher state maps and local signs on trips which sometimes ranged over thousands of miles. I learned to pull a trailer at a young age too. That way, my Dad would pull the boat, while I pulled the pop-up camper that they eventually bought. On long trips, when we were only taking the camper, I would often drive while Dad slept in the back sleep.

I felt important on these trips. It was like my Dad noticed me and appreciated my abilities to navigate and drive. I felt like his partner in planning the whole trip or the day's adventures. It built my confidence to travel to various places and because of that I have taken many car trips alone. I have driven to Boston and Louisiana by myself, totally capable of planning my trip and finding my way. As a teacher I had the summer off, so I sub-let my apartment in Ohio, drove to Florida, and traveled from place to place. I would stay a week or so at a time and traveled throughout the state for the entire summer! People were amazed that as a woman I would have the courage to go by myself. But I had no qualms about being able to find my way around and take care of myself in various cities and situations.

As an adult, I continued going on vacations with my parents for many years. My first husband, Jay, and I bought a tent and camped right along with my relatives for several years. It was fun to continue the traditions and tell stories and share pictures of all our experiences. After my divorce, I would continue to go on vacations with my folks. My Mom worked at the same school where I taught, so we would have summers off along with the same week for spring break. The three of us would travel together to the eastern coast or go down to Florida and enjoy the warm weather after our long Ohio winters. One year, my folks planned a trip with another couple to the Bahamas over spring break. I wanted to go, too! The other couple had a single adult daughter also, so she and I talked it over and decided to room together in Nassau. We ate some meals with our folks but had lots of time to discover the island for ourselves and enjoy the nightlife too.

Another trip that I took with them one summer was to the Atlantic seashore. We rented a large 4-bedroom condo with two other couples, Aunt Shirley and Uncle John & his sister and brother-in-law, Sandra and Rob. There was a large central area for the open kitchen and living room which looked out onto the ocean. There were two bedrooms on either side of this main living space with a shared bathroom between each bedroom. I had one bedroom to myself and shared the bath with my folks' adjoining bedroom. We had a wonderful time creating giant meals, playing on the beach and doing the typical tourist shopping. But one event in particular stands out from that vacation.

There was one day when we were all getting ready to go out and eat. We had all showered and our bedroom doors were closed. Mom had finished getting ready and was in the main living area while I was in my bedroom and Dad was putting on his shirt in their bedroom. I needed new batteries for my camera, so I went through our shared bathroom and knocked on his bedroom door. I asked if he had any spare batteries and he gave me a couple. I sat down on their bed, loading the batteries in my camera while Dad finished getting ready. Well, Mom heard us both in her bedroom behind the closed door and came bursting in the door screaming, "What are you two doing in here? Stop it!"

I looked up from the camera in my lap and Dad turned around from the mirror where he was combing his hair. I looked at her curiously and wondered what she was talking about. What did she think was happening?

I asked her "What do you mean? I'm putting batteries in my camera. What did you think we were doing in here, Mom?"

She looked at each of us and realized that the situation was quite harmless.

"Mom!" I said, "What did you mean by 'What are we doing in here?'" She was red in the face and panting.

"Nothing," she said, "Nothing."

"Why did you tell us to stop?" I asked her, now standing looking at the two of them. She ran out of the room, so I looked at Dad. He just started laughing and making fun of Mom saying something like 'There goes your crazy Mother again." He was so good at shedding the whole situation and blaming the awkwardness and tension on her. The memories of the sexual abuse were still deeply buried in me, so I never knew what that situation was really about and was left wondering over the years what she meant. But eventually, I would know exactly what she meant. My question now is that why was she suspicious of me and Dad, even though I was now an adult. Did she really still think that there was something sexual going on between my father and me? Did she really see me as competition with her? That I was doing something behind her back? Is that the way she saw the abuse…not that it was something being done TO me, but rather it was something I was actively taking part in? It was something happening behind closed doors by us that was actually being done to hurt HER? I'll never really know.

I thank my parents for traveling with us kids. It exposed me to many other lifestyles and I got to see many, many beautiful places in this country. I grew to appreciate the outdoors and it instilled in me the desire to enjoy nature and take care of it.

I've shared some of the details of my life growing up to show you how close I was to my parents. I shared many activities with them, even vacations during my adult life. And yet, I didn't remember the abuse. The memories were repressed very solidly from my consciousness.

The Façade is Cracking

Growing up in my family was a complex field of situations and emotions. We had fun on vacations and on the weekend camping trips, but there was an underlying uneasiness that permeated the air.

When I was young, I had a deep understanding that I was alone. Completely alone. I had no guardian in the house, no protector. My Mom was abused herself and had never received help to overcome the feelings of shame and weakness and low self worth. She needed my Dad to feel worthy, to feel that she mattered at all in this world. Without him, she was nothing—literally nothing. To be recognized by him, noticed by him, somewhat loved by him, it gave her worth. Without him she was invisible. She was no one of notice. That feeling of being invisible is something I can now relate to. It's like when the abuse is happening, you become numb. No one sees you, the real you. When the abuse is over, no one talks about it, so it feels like the whole thing doesn't really exist—like it's another world or dimension that no one else can see. It's an invisible world and so you begin to think that you're invisible. In the real everyday world then, you try to get someone to notice you. I needed to be noticed to feel like I existed, to feel that I was real.

So I took on different behaviors to get noticed. I was the perfect child at home - never in trouble, never causing a ruckus. I was also the perfect child in school, loved by teachers, fantastic grades, overachiever, overly helping folks to make sure they liked me and wanted me around. I was always anticipating what others may have needed or wanted and getting it for them just when they needed it. I became so codependent on what others thought of me. I needed people's attention in order to create a sense of self-worth, a sense that when I was around folks, they would notice me which validated that it was happening, that is was real. And so as I got older, my codependency continued into my relationships. I always did things to make other people happy. I never considered doing things to make myself happy. There were many activities where I was enjoying the time and activity, but my goal was to make others happy so that they would like me. If they liked me, then I was worthy of being alive. My self-esteem would get a boost because I could make people laugh, or make them comfortable, or make them feel good about themselves. If I could accomplish that, then I was a good person. I didn't know that I was doing this pattern of thinking and behaving at the time. But when I was 19, I went to a weekend personal growth retreat that a college friend invited me to attend. At that retreat, one of the facilitators asked everyone what they really wanted in life. Everyone in the group, every single person in the circle had goals and aspirations. I had a blank sheet in my mind. Not one thought, not one, came to my mind as to what I wanted out of my life. Yes I knew I wanted to be a teacher. That was a given. I knew I would become a teacher when I was very small. But the thought of what else I wanted, I had never thought about it before. Nobody had ever asked me that before. My life revolved around making friends happy, my parents happy, my extended family happy. But I never thought about what would make me happy! No one in my family had ever asked me that before and I had never asked myself that before.

The retreat happened to be held on the same weekend as our annual family reunion. I had attended the retreat on Friday evening and all day Saturday, and if I went to the Sunday sessions, I would have to miss the family reunion. I felt very guilty about missing the reunion and knew my folks would be disappointed. To help ease my guilt I went to the picnic shelter early Sunday morning to help decorate. I made lots of food for the reunion, even though I would eat none of it. When I told my Mom I would not be coming to the reunion that day she was furious with me. I explained that I was attending a personal growth seminar and that it was important to me. She and my dad yelled at me and called me selfish and self-centered, that I would miss a reunion and go do something that was just for me. This was more reaction than I expected and I felt really hurt by their comments and name calling. I had helped at every holiday, birthday, reunion, and many other family gatherings over the years. But this one Sunday I wanted to attend something different and I was being accused of not loving my family.

This was how my parents continued to control me. They further minimized the worth of me—that I should always sacrifice my happiness for them. "I" was never worthy of exploring.

Something dramatic changed that weekend. I left the picnic shelter and went back to the retreat crying all the way, feeling angry and surprised. Feeling like I had to break away—I didn't know what I was breaking away from, or why. Why were they so angry when I gave and gave all the time? I even gave that day—going early to hang decorations and preparing food. But my total allegiance was demanded. The individual was never important. The façade of the happy family was ultimate. And this was the first crack in the façade! I didn't know that then. While at the retreat later that day and within the group session I explained the reactions of my parents to the other participants. It was the first time I felt like I questioned their love for me and sensed the dysfunction of our family. I was stepping out of the acceptable mode of behavior and trying something introspective and self-nurturing, and my parents were furious.

My parents couldn't even explain why they were so angry. They didn't know themselves well enough to be able to see their control issues and the fear they lived in. I had never really stepped outside the boundaries of "acceptable" behavior before. I had always done the right thing. I had always attended and joyfully helped at every event. I had always overlooked my personal desires in order to do things for the family. So it surprised me greatly to hear them say that I didn't love them or didn't care about family. It was astonishing to hear them call me selfish and uncaring! Their explosive reaction was greatly exaggerated for missing one family gathering and this wasn't an especially important reunion—like a grandparent's 50th anniversary or a wedding reception. It was just a big family picnic like we had every year. And yet, their reaction and anger and accusations were as if I was blowing off an epic day in our family history or had done something horrific to embarrass the family.

I responded to their accusations of "You don't love your family!" with a blank stare, big eyes and a gaping mouth. All I could utter was "What?" How could I be accused of that after all I've done in the past. It didn't make sense. What you did in the past didn't matter. You had to prove your love and allegiance over and over again. I cried and I argued with them, but I did go to the retreat. That day, I gained a backbone. And it felt miserable, but it felt like my survival depended on it. There was such a strong drive to attend this retreat and learn about new ways of thinking and new ways of developing the self. I don't remember the name of the retreat or where it was held, or the friend who invited me, but it changed my life. I sincerely thank that friend. This incident holds an important piece of wisdom—you never know how a small comment you make to a friend, how a class you may teach to a group, or how a book you recommend to a stranger may make a difference in their life. The ripple effect of our actions—the loving comment, the group discussion you hold, the peaceful meditation you lead—it may have a wonderful effect on someone and you may never be aware of your impact. And some day, someone will look back and remember that you were the person who changed their thinking, made them more aware of their own inner light, or gave them a soothing comment or hug to help them on their journey.

We are all connected and our words and actions are so powerful. Choose your words kindly and carefully. Give lots of hugs and loving looks and gestures to others. It tells them you notice them. Kind words and caring ways show people they're not invisible. You noticed them and cared enough to share a smile, took a minute to listen, extended a gesture of concern—each act tells someone they're not alone and not invisible. Your compassion tells them that they matter. You, as an earthly representation of God, show them they matter.

The Nightmares

During my late twenties and early thirties, I lived alone. At night, I would often have a terrible nightmare that would awaken me and leave me feeling like there was an intruder in my bedroom. In my dream, I could see the silhouette of a man standing in my bedroom doorway, a light shining behind him that accented his figure. He was coming to get me and I awoke just as he entered my bedroom. I would sit straight up in bed terrified that a man was in my room. My heart would be pounding when I woke from this horrible recurring dream. I would be breathing hard and sweating profusely. The dream was so real!

I had this nightmare many, many times over the years. I attributed it to the fact that I was a single woman living alone in a downtown apartment. I usually felt safe living there, but rationalized that the nightmare was caused by an underlying element of fear or tension in me because the undesirable neighborhoods weren't all that far away from me. I would wake up from this dream panting and scared shitless, feeling like someone was in my home and just about to rape me. I would look to the doorway and see no one there and slowly start breathing normal again. My racing heartbeat would gradually resume its natural rhythm as I convinced myself that I was safe. I often would get up and turn on all the lights in the apartment just to make sure I was alone, and sometimes even wash my armpits because of the intense sweating I had experienced. I had never told my therapist about these dreams. I simply wrote them off as a typical fear of a single woman living alone.

I had been seeing a therapist for my depression and thoughts of suicide. During one counseling session, my therapist suggested that she thought I may have been sexually abused by my father. I was surprised by what she said. I told her that I didn't remember any type of sexual abuse, just the verbal, physical and mental abuse that she and I had discussed in previous sessions.

That very night I had the same dream again. I'm sleeping in my bed and a man is standing in the bedroom doorway with a light shining from behind creating a dark silhouette of his shape. I woke up in terror again, sitting straight up in bed, breathing hard, heart pounding and scared shitless, just like all the other times I had had this nightmare. But this time I screamed, "No, Daddy!"

I now started trembling from a new kind of shock. My mind raced with questions. *What the hell was that? What did I just say? Where did that come from? What does that mean? Why did I say that?*

The recurring nightmares had simply been my sub-conscious mind trying to put me in touch with the truth. The repressed memories wanted out. The memories, images and feelings of the abuse started flooding my reality throughout the months to come. Memories of him touching me, being naked with me, holding me down, beating me, and threatening me into submission, all came back. Some memories were brief pictures, like still snapshots, while others were like video clips where the scene played out in my mind in detail. And when these images, still or moving, came into my consciousness, I was overwhelmed, not just by the pictures I saw, but by the tremendous feelings of being a child and of being attacked.

I was to learn in further counseling sessions and from books that when your brain buries the memory of an event, it also blocks the emotions that you were feeling right then. It somehow takes the whole event and shrink-wraps it for storage. It allows you to somehow separate from what is happening so that it doesn't harm the very soul of you. But then when you open the package, everything comes out so that you feel you're actually living it again.

I would feel that I was six years old and someone's fingers were being forced inside my tiny vagina. Or I would feel like I was ten years old and naked and being whipped with a leather belt before the sexual abuse was about to begin. The pain and the fear, the hopelessness and the loneliness, the anguish—all of it was inside my head and body again. The feeling of having no control over my body—the anger and greed of the man—could be felt inside me to my very core. The feeling of being screamed at and told that I'm ugly and worthless came flooding back. I could hear his voice telling me that no one would ever want me now.

It was so important to know how to control these surfacing memories, so that I could look at them and deal with them at appropriate and safe times. I hold such gratitude for my counselors and fellow group members for helping me survive the reliving of these memories. It's an ugly part of the healing process, but an important, essential, un-skippable step in getting whole.

These memories contain the information you need to make you feel safe and sane. They fill in the missing pieces. They explain why you are the way you are. The memories help explain why you react so acutely to certain situations or smells or objects. For me it explained why I am so afraid of guns and men's leather belts. It isn't necessary to open every single shrink-wrapped package, but enough of them need to be exposed to understand the situations and all their ramifications. I also learned that it's very common for women in their early thirties to start remembering these painful, buried memories.

The memories seemed to surface in layers for me—each layer exposing a new truth or set of circumstances that would help in my healing process. First, it would reveal my age level when the abuse took place or the location where it occurred. The memories may later show me the violence, or the threat of violence, that was used to force me to comply and stay silent. The memories would eventually reveal to me that my mother knew of the abuse all along, in fact, it would show me the very conversation I had with her at the age of 4, asking her to make him stop, and she chose to do nothing about it. That revelation would bring up its own set of feelings of grief and anger.

And all of the memories are good. Each ugly, exhausting, resurfacing memory is good in its own way. Each memory brought information that I needed in order to eventually be okay. And once the memory surfaced, once I relived the feelings and discussed them in the individual or group counseling sessions, the impact of the emotional drain would lessen. To relive it was to relieve it!

The memory will never go away, but the emotional attachment will fade until you can look at the abuse objectively and not feel the pain so acutely. I can talk about a particular occurrence of the abuse now and not feel the rage and resentment and fear that once accompanied the memory. It may feel uncomfortable and bring a sense of sadness at times for me, but I'm not in the clutches of the volatile, maddening emotions I once felt.

I didn't see the good in all of this at the time, but I trusted the therapists and workshop participants. They all told me it was therapeutic, that I needed to do this. It sure didn't feel good. In fact, it felt damn lousy. But I was determined to take my life back. I wanted to heal from the things that had damaged my psyche and be a whole, healthy woman. I was determined not to let the abuse affect the rest of my life. My father had stolen my childhood from me, left me feeling unworthy and shameful throughout my teens, twenties and early thirties, but I was damned sure he wasn't going to ruin and control the rest of my entire life. I would heal! I would recover! I would thrive! And someday, I would be happy! As we often said in group therapy, "Recovery is the best revenge."

And I have recovered. I am happy. I have a wonderful healthy relationship with a man. I have hope for even better things as I continue to heal. This is a process—a process that never ends, but gets easier along the way.

Counseling

Thoughts create emotions. Thoughts create things.
Counseling helps people who have been abused change their thoughts. Therapy helped me change my thoughts about myself, my family, the abuse, and the world at large. I thought of myself as being bright, fairly attractive, and outgoing. But deep inside me, I thought of myself as being a phony. I thought that I was really not a very good person. The shame from the abuse colored my perception of myself. I projected to the world an image of being happy, competent, and confident, but inside I was really very shaky, sad and uncertain. I felt less than everyone else. I felt very different, like I didn't belong. So I tried very hard to belong.

During my teens, twenties, and thirties, I was drawn to harlequin masks. They showed a beautiful clown face, adorned in jewels and feathers, and beads. The colors were often very vibrant and bright, but sometimes very subtle and feminine. But no matter what the colors or adornments, there was always one tear flowing down the cheek. Of course, I never knew why I was drawn to these masks. Maybe they reminded me of the Mardi Gras Festival in New Orleans, a festival I have always wanted to attend. Or maybe it appealed to my love for Halloween parties. I love to don costumes and play make-believe for a night. It was always fun to step out of my usual role and play Wonder Woman or Cleopatra for an evening. But little did I know that the harlequin mask was actually my real face. It wasn't pretend at all. I did project a happy and outgoing persona to the world around me. I was sometimes colorful and vibrant and sometimes soft and feminine. But I always had a tear running down my cheek. The inside sadness was always there.

INDIVIDUAL COUNSELING

My counselors certainly helped change my thoughts. Their guidance and insights helped me change my viewpoint about relationships in the outer world, and more importantly, the relationship with myself in my inner world. One of the best changes that happened was my release of the need to be perfect. My inner world was so unstable and chaotic and I didn't want anyone to see it. So, I felt the need to be perfect in everything I did. I felt that if someone saw something that was out of place or if I made an error, people would find out about me and know that I was a fraud. The inner feeling of not being real, not being authentic, was a driving force in my need to impress everyone.

Let me give you some examples. Because of the underlying feeling of unworthiness, I never went out of the house without my hair done perfectly and my make-up applied just right. Even a run to the local convenient store meant changing clothes, putting on or checking my make-up, and fixing my hair just so. I had to make the outer shell appear completely okay to the local cashier. Like he or she even cared! I had to appear perfect to everyone around. Another prime example is with my kitchen trash can. If I had a date in the evening, or was having friends over to watch a video, I would clean my house, as anyone would normally do. You know, straighten up the living room, clean the kitchen and generally dust and run the vacuum. But my obsession with the kitchen trash can was way out there. Throughout the day of cleaning, I would throw away the old newspapers, get rid of the junk mail, maybe throw out the moldy leftovers in the refrigerator, and clean the cat's litter box. All normal stuff, right? When you're done, you take the bag out of the wastebasket, tie it up with a twisty-tie, and take the bag out to the garbage can. I'd put a clean bag in the kitchen waste can and under the kitchen sink it would go. Now here's the weird part: it had to stay that way until my company would come over. The trash can **had** to be absolutely empty when my guests arrived. If I found something else that needed to be thrown away, I would freak out. And I'm not talking about putting something smelly or rude in the trash can either like the cat's litter. It could be a paper towel that I just used to clean the bathroom mirror or the packaging from a box of macaroni. My thoughts about myself were so reliant on other people's opinion of me that I could not have any trash in the kitchen. I had to be perfect in order for people to think of me as being okay. I truly believed that if I had trash in my trash can, people would think less of me. How pitiful is that. Is that how you pick your friends? By the amount of garbage they have in their can? Maybe in a way, I thought of myself as trash or garbage, something used and dirty to be thrown away and discarded. I don't know what the obsession really is based on, but the counseling helped me see how my need to be perfect was running, and ruining, my life.

My need to be perfect also affected my relationships. I had to be right all the time. I had to be the one who was always in the know. I had to give the perfect directions, pick the perfect present and wrap it just perfectly. I had to pick the right restaurant, teach the perfect class…everyday, and receive the highest grades or honors or reviews from everything I attempted. There was no such thing in my life as good enough. It had to be perfect! And making a mistake was just plain inexcusable. If I made an error, I would chastise myself with I should have known better, tried harder, or been more vigilant. The self-condemnation was way worse than anything anyone else ever said to me. I was embarrassed of myself when I made a mistake and heaped on all the ridicule and scorn that I could muster. With counseling, I realized just how much I didn't like myself.

One of the common homework assignments given by my

counselors was to write down the comments that I told myself in my head. Sheesh! I uncovered a ton of nasty internal dialogues that were going on inside me. The self-talk was full of contempt and disapproval. When I realized how nasty I was to myself, no wonder I felt bad all the time. Would I ever talk that way to another person? No way! And yet I piled on the judgments in huge bucketfuls. I prided myself for always being encouraging and hopeful with my students when they made a mistake. And yet I allowed no room for errors for myself. I was ruthless. I then was asked to look at my list of self-inflicted comments and consider a friend saying those things to me. Would I keep that friend around? No way! So why would I allow myself, my ego, to talk to me that way?

The counseling I received and the self-help books I read were extremely helpful in changing my thoughts. My critical parent voice was quieted for the most part. My life became more peaceful without the incessant criticisms and put-downs in my head. My obsession with being perfect eased and I found it easier to be around people. I'm even able to have trash in my kitchen garbage can now when folks come over! But regardless of the work I did on myself, I still felt an underlying sense of not being okay. Regardless of having two college degrees, I felt I still was less than other people—not quite whole. I felt inadequate like I had something to hide from people. The shame was still there.

This is where spirituality entered my life and I was able to shed that shame. I started understanding that I was a spiritual being having a human experience. I was a spiritual being before I got here on Earth—perfect in every way. Inside this human, five foot five inch shell resides that spirit—still perfect in every way. The human side of me might make mistakes as I navigate through relationships, career choices, credit cards, and healthy eating, but the true me is still perfect. I am here on this planet, at this time, to experience situations and discover my power as a spirit-filled being.

One of the purposes of this life for me is to be truly authentic. My goal is to be real and present for every moment of life, to be the same person whether in private with Wayne or a close friend, or in public with coworkers and strangers. My goal is to never pretend anymore that everything's just fine. The trick for me was being able to be real and still have friends and a job. I was so afraid to be real before because I needed people's approval so much. Now, I was taking the chance of being honest with myself and with others. I was going to speak my truth and be real about what was happening in my life. I was taking off the mask and that was damn scary! What if no one liked me? What if everyone left me? The fear of being abandoned was terrifying. But as my counselors pointed out, people who liked me now liked a fake. And as Dr. Phil would say, "How's that working for you?" It wasn't working, so I tried being another way.

Learning how to be real was tricky. I had to speak my mind honestly, but I had to learn how to do it in a loving way so that everyone felt respected. My buried anger and resentments often made my comments have a harsh edge to them. I learned how to use "I statements," instead of the accusatory "You statements." I was impatient at times with people; in fact, this is still an area I'm working on. I learned how to listen, really listen to someone else's opinion. I took the time to process their views, instead of creating my response while they were talking. To speak the truth in a caring way, setting boundaries, asking for what you want and still have friends is a delicate balance of being truthful and being kind. I learned how to respond to people and situations, instead of reacting out of fear and anger.

As I became even slightly more aware of my perfect spirit inside, my confidence grew. I became more peaceful and secure. And as I became more authentic, I attracted more authentic people to me. The shallow people I used to congregate with started falling away. For a while, I had very few close friends and at times I felt very alone. This is a normal circumstance for anyone who is leaving an old lifestyle behind and adopting a new way of being. Those who are leaving addictions of any kind know this to be true as well. As I became more real, I grew bored with people who constantly talked about their designer clothes or on the other end complained incessantly about their lousy lot in life. In fact, I saw them as good people who were desperate for attention, just as I had been. I joined a class that studied a book called *A Course in Miracles* and met many people who were on a spiritual journey like mine. I met people who hungered for more information about the Truth of who they really were, and were willing to look at their own behaviors and thought patterns. These folks were willing to look deep inside and discern their spirit from their ego and make loving changes in themselves as they progressed.

I especially parted with people who were judgmental and pretentious. I found that folks who carried strong feelings of superiority against people of other races, religions, and sexual orientations became increasingly distasteful. Their harsh judgments and blanket statements about stereotypes were offensive. Those who were insensitive to the plights of others dropped away from my circle of friends. And in their place came a wonderful group of people with compassion, joy and higher consciousness. I learned so much from these new friends. Our discussions led me to new concepts to learn and new books to read. Their compassion and love are what have led me to where I am now. Their suggestions have actually led me to write this book.

Group therapy

While doing my individual therapy sessions, I became aware of a local support group in the area called Survivors of Sexual Abuse. I asked my counselor about the dynamics of group therapy, how it worked and if it was effective. She described it as a way to share my experiences with others who had similar circumstances. Group therapy was a method of learning from each other, under the care and guidance of a license counselor. It was one additional tool to use for hearing. It sounded perfect! I met with the counselor who led the survivor's group, Sondra Fronimo, to determine if the group would be beneficial to me. I loved her from the start. She was so laid back and kind. Here was a woman who was herself a victim of sexual abuse by her father and a true survivor. During our initial meeting, we discussed my background and the few memories that had surfaced, my counseling session with my other therapist, and my goals for attending the group sessions. I would continue to see my therapist on a regular basis and attend the weekly survivor's group. The met on Thursday evenings right after work. I started the group therapy immediately.

The Survivor's Group met in the Board room of a social service agency and we would push the large 15-foot table off to a corner and bring the chairs around in a circle. We had a small wall-mounted whiteboard that was available for Sondra to make notes or diagrams on. But mostly we just talked. On that very first meeting I didn't know what to expect. Would we all sit around telling our personal horror stories? Would I connect with anyone? The first meeting was such a relief! I met 6 other wonderful women, all in different stages of healing. We talked about so many topics and issues that I took three pages of notes! The format for the meeting would be that Sondra would open up by saying "How's everyone doing?" Someone in the group would offer a story of an event or situation that was giving her problems in her life. From that story, Sondra and the others would give feedback on what they heard her say, would address the larger issues surrounding the event or story and possibly offer advice for handling the situation. From the stories told, here are some of the things we discussed on my very first day:

- People who have been victimized:
    - feel **everyone** must like them
    - will not set healthy limits or boundaries
    - have to please everyone
    - always explain their behavior
    - are always caretaking others
    - are hyper-vigilent
- Learn to use "I" statements rather than "You" sentences
- Trust your gut feeling; Victims negate their intuition and allow others to discount their feelings.

- Victims have an unrealistic need to control
- How to change the need to be liked
- What does love mean to victims
- Issues of trust
- Look at a picture of myself as a child; get to see how small and helpless I was; Helps relieve guilt
- What was life like for my mother?

I found a way to learn about myself from other people who had been through this. These were brave women who shared their grief and mistakes. They let me look at their behaviors, which were sometimes outlandish and embarrassing, and see inside their heads, to view their thoughts. They let me inside their hearts, where all the dark feelings resided. I grew to deeply love this group of women and their ability to share their darkest thoughts and raw emotions. They let me watch as they healed. And eventually I let them look at my behaviors and my weak self-image. I let them into my darkest thoughts and very real emotions. And they watched as I healed. This is where I first learned to be really authentic. The trust that was shared by those in the group was simply remarkable. Phone numbers were shared with each other, so that we could call upon each other during the week in times of need. It was an open entry/open exit group meaning that the door was always open to newcomers and that a woman could leave whenever she felt she was ready to handle life on her own. This type of policy was very beneficial for many reasons. First, you didn't have to wait for a new class to start in order to join. There were almost always openings. Secondly, there wasn't an end to the class nor did anyone tell you when you were done. You left when you felt you didn't need the group anymore. Also, it was very encouraging over time to see how folks progressed. Healing is often very slow and subtle. So when I would see a woman who just joined the group blubbering over how she had never told anyone about the abuse before, I felt her pain but could also see how far I had come. I could see my old self in the pathetic, almost lifeless woman sitting across from me and note how much I had learned and healed. It was during the next two years I watched women come into our group as sobbing blobs of human flesh and turn into divine creatures able to hold their head up with pride, knowing they had the ability to take care of themselves.

I found it so interesting the types of personalities that were in the group. There were those like me who were confident and self-assured on the outside, successful women who were scared and shaky on the inside. Others were shy and reclusive, almost wishing they couldn't be seen. There were those who were sexually promiscuous, those who were functionally fairly well sexually, those who were frigid, and those who were still virgins in their 30's and 40's. Some of us were married, some single, and some divorced. Many, if not most, of the women had had problems with unhealthy relationships with men. Most of us were terrible at taking care of ourselves.

One of the most important things I learned from the survivors group was how fear was the primary emotion that controlled the lives of survivors of sexual abuse. This certainly goes along with what we are taught in *A Course in Miracles*. In this wonderful book, we learn there are really only two emotions: love and fear. In all situations, we choose to view the world through a filter of either love or fear. This filter colors all experiences and all of our interpretations of the world. Do we respond out of love or react out of fear? And we view ourselves with either love or fear also. If we view ourselves with love, we listen to our intuition, we care for ourselves by eating nutritional meals, getting enough rest and relaxation, and surrounding ourselves with kind and loving people. When we live through the eyes of fear, we doubt or ignore our intuition, have poor personal boundaries and do things that are not always in our own best interest. We go along with the crowd, no matter how uncomfortable or unhealthy something may be, because we fear being alone or rejected.

As a victim, I was fearful of the fact that my body would fail me. I was afraid that I was weak and I would not be able to take care of myself. As the adult survivor, I often blamed myself for not being stronger to fight off my father. My rational mind knew that he was a grown man and I was a small five year old girl. But somehow, I still blamed my body for not protecting me. I also feared that my body would betray me in letting my father think that I liked what he was doing to me. My father would often stimulate my clitoris and make me have an orgasm. It somehow helped him rationalize that what he was doing was pleasurable for me too. When I would come, he would say, "See, you like this too." It didn't matter that I would be struggling against him or crying or simply limp from giving up, he saw the orgasm as a way to relieve his guilt. My body would betray me. In reality, it simply did what it was built to do—respond to touch. Even though I hated what was happening when he was in my bed, I felt fear that my body would act in a way that wasn't true to what was going on in my heart and mind.

I also feared my gut feelings or intuition. As a child, I knew that what was happening in my family was wrong. It was crazy behavior and felt confusing and unsafe. But everyone in the family and community acted as if none of this was happening. How could I trust what I was feeling when no one seemed to notice the insanity. I feared that my intuition was wrong or not to be trusted to distinguish the truth. I doubted my ability to discern situations. I developed a distorted reality. I feared my ability to distinguish trustworthy people, to tell the difference between loving and non-loving behaviors. I feared me. I didn't feel I could be trusted to distinguish the truth.

So from this fear of the world outside of me and fearing the world inside of me, I developed a pattern of reacting to situations with anger. Rather than simply responding to my surroundings, I would criticize or rebuke. I wasn't physically abusive. I was too small and weak for that. My weapon of choice was the spoken word. I am bright and I have a large vocabulary. So, I used it on people. I diminished people with a word or a look or a tone of voice. I was excellent at controlling people, which was quite useful when teaching 180 junior high students each day. But it wasn't a good tactic to use with other adults. My typical response would be to verbally attack someone and then in private, sulk and play the event over and over in my head. I would play the victim role to the hilt. Oh poor, pitiful me. Why does everything always happen to me? I would then feel weak and fearful going out into the world again and feel like I had to be tough to protect myself.

Because of this, victims often don't associate with their bodies. They disconnect from their bodies.

I'm going through my notebook that I kept during the survivors group. I'm surprised as I look through my notes to find a page about Louise Hay. I had no idea that this enlightened thinking was presented to me back in 1989! I wrote "Healing tape by Louise Hay" in my notes, so I'm not sure if it was an audio tape that we listened to or a video tape that we watched. But my notes are full of the wonderful truths that I now 'know' deep within me. There started my spiritual journey of healing and I didn't even remember it. I have written in my notebook, "Change your thoughts that create the feelings of guilt and shame. Shame keeps us a victim." Louise states that we must forgive in order to heal. Just saying, "I am willing to forgive," will start the process. Thank you Sondra, for introducing me to Louise Hay and using her wonderful teachings so long ago!

Part III:
The Sacred Heart

The Sacred Heart

As I sat quietly in meditation today, a picture formed in my mind's eye. It is of a heart with three circles around it. I can't see all the details yet, but I've learned to just wait and let things come into view. I often receive a vision of a picture or graphic when I meditate and today was no different. This picture, I was being told, was a depiction of the Sacred Heart and the damage that is done to our Spirit when we are sexually abused. I'm told that this graphic will be very useful in my book as we explore the types of damage that is done to us by sexual abuse. It will also help us discover various ways we can repair that damage.

As the image comes into focus, I see the Sacred Heart is located within three overlapping circles. One circle represents the Mind, the second circle is for the Body, and the third circle symbolizes the Spirit. When someone is mentally abused, the Mind Circle gets a dent in it. When someone is physically abused, the Body Circle receives a dent. The Spirit Circle is dented when someone receives a blow to their self-worth.

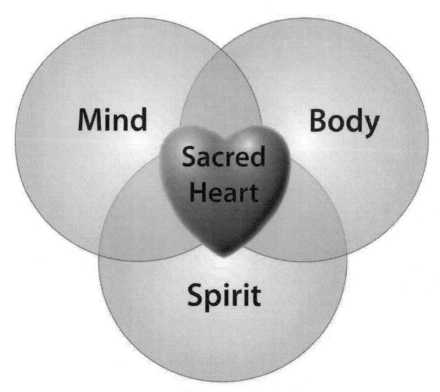

The Sacred Heart.

The devastating truth about sexual abuse is that it affects all three areas at the same time. Sexual abuse affects the Mind, the Body, and the Spirit of a person. They are devastating blows to the very essence of what makes us a human being. We are a package deal—Mind, Body and Spirit. Our Mind consists of our ego, our personality, and it is damaged by the sexual abuse. Our Body is the physical component of us that is being attacked and violated by our abuser. Our Spirit is our own inner Light, our essence that is our connection with God. That Light is diminished when we have been sexually attacked. This wonderful picture I received beautifully illustrated how all of these parts make up our Sacred Heart and how sexual abuse dents or damages all three components of our being.

With all of these dents in our Mind, Body, Spirit fields surrounding our Sacred Heart, we begin to feel that we are less than others. We feel less than normal, less worthy, less deserving, less meaningful, less attractive, less smart, less capable, less womanly/manly. In reality, we're not any of these things, but we feel less than others. And here lies the core of the problem. This feeling of being 'less than' shapes all of our behavior, all of our thinking, all of our actions, all of our reactions. We don't even know that we're viewing the world and responding to the world from this limited, damaged, albeit incorrect, perspective. We're blind to the fact that we think we're less than everyone else. We feel we're damaged goods. We feel inferior, but we have no idea how deep our problem lies and what can make us feel good again. For some who have buried all memories of their abuse, like I did, we don't even know why we feel different, why we don't fit in or feel normal.

We go about our lives trying to fill the dents from the outside so that we're whole and pretty! We try a variety of different behaviors and substances to fill the gaps in our armor, the crinkled rusted dents in our Sacred Heart. We try drugs and alcohol to fill in the dents, like putty on a car or spackling on a piece of drywall. Maybe gambling or shopping will make us feel better…will make us feel important and attractive. Indiscriminate sex and dysfunctional relationships all try to fill the emptiness that we feel inside. We use any relationship, no matter how superficial or destructive it is, to try to fill in the empty spaces and the dents caused by the abuse. We keep trying so hard to fill in the dents in order to feel whole. We're tired of feeling incomplete and less than everyone else. We just want to feel right.

We may feel the need to over-achieve in order to compensate for our feelings of inadequacy. We work hard to make more money, achieve good grades, make the sale, impress our boss or surpass our neighbors and co-workers. We grab onto power and dominate others cruelly. We think that if we are above others, then we are not less than them. We continue to search for things on the OUTSIDE that can fill us—fill the dents, fill the empty feelings, and make us whole. We keep searching for something that will finally make us feel okay about ourselves.

Or sometimes we loathe ourselves so much, we continue the

abuse and add more dents to ourselves. We add dents to our Body circle as we perform some type of self-mutilation, practice some form of eating disorder like anorexia, bulimia or gluttony, or attract and stay in relationships that bring us violence and drama. We feel this is all we deserve because we ARE less than others, of course, and this is the best we can do. We take in excessive amounts of alcohol and drugs to hide the pain, but instead add more dents to our physical bodies. Our self-talk is critical and demeaning as we continue to add dents to the Mind circle. Our Spirit is deflated again and again as we stay in relationships where people put us down and ridicule our behaviors. There are dents from our abusers and even more dents from ourselves. We don't make healthy choices because we don't think we're worth it.

But our true healing from the abuse does not come from the outside. Our true healing must come from the inside. Psychotherapy is a wonderful tool for recovery and I urge you to find a trained counselor to help you navigate these waters. I probably wouldn't be alive had it not been for my wonderful, effective counselors. But I found that therapy could only take me so far. It dealt mostly with the mind and the emotions, but not the spirit. I wanted to heal all of me, the whole being – all components of the Sacred Heart. Eventually, I found that I could heal from within, from my own spirit, from my own Light and vibration.

When we look within and acknowledge the Sacred Heart, the very soul of us, we start to grow! We learn to love ourselves and slowly realize that we are perfect inside. The dents are still there but the sexual abuse didn't hurt my very soul. Most of us, including me, didn't even know that we had a Sacred Heart—a holy center that is of God. At the first suggestion of a holy Light within me, I shrugged and said "Yeah, Right!" I had been told too many times by my father that I was no good and that no one would want me. And I believed it.

I had also been told by the Baptist Church that I was filled with original sin and headed for damnation. The idea that I was a Holy Light was a joke.

I knew I was a good person. Somehow I knew that much. But I still felt less than everyone else, inadequate at some level that I couldn't quite identify. So I continued with my self-defeating behaviors, my never ending negative self-talk, and my dead-end relationships. I continued to feel sad and lonely.

My outer shell, the Mind, Body, Spirit circles, were banged up pretty bad. There were plenty of dents from the sexual abuse, the verbal abuse, the physical abuse, the bad relationships, the religious teachings, and the self-inflicted blows. But the Sacred Heart within us is strong and resilient. Thank God! No matter what happens on the outside or inside of us, no matter what our mind is thinking, the Sacred Heart still resides within us, whole and strong. The essence of who we really are exists within the circles perfect and whole. It's just that no one has ever told us that it's there. Our Spirit may have been diminished to a tiny spark, but it is always there. It only needs to be acknowledged to start growing. The Spirit needs only to feel your belief and the healing starts. The Spirit needs only to feel our hope that there is a Spirit. As our belief grows, the Spirit grows. As the Spirit grows, the dents are popped out from the inside. One by one the slightest dimples start turning back out. The spirit softly pushes out the dents and brings us back to wholeness. One by one, softening the evidence of the abuse, our Spirit is eased into the Light of wonder and the glow of health. Mental health. Physical Health. Spiritual Health. Emotional Health. As we raise our vibration inside, everything within us starts operating on a different level. And the true healing begins.

The dents will always have a slight mar on the outer surface of the circles surrounding our Sacred Heart. We can never pretend that the abuse didn't happen and that it has all magically gone away. It is a part of us, just like going to the 2nd grade is a part of us. It's an experience that has shaped us. But we have the power inside our Sacred Heart to reshape us. The Light within is stronger than any dent. It can all be restored by going within and focusing on the Light of the Divine that is within each of us.

How do we go within? There are many routes to our Sacred

Heart and you'll need to find the one that's just right for you. I prefer to use many options to go within, just as I like to take different roads when I drive home from work. I may see something different or learn something new from changing my route and the same is true when exploring your inner landscape. There is so much to learn and so many wonderful things to explore as you find out how wonderful you are!

The Sacred Heart is your special connection to God, to the one Great Spirit who knows all, heals all, and loves us all. The Sacred Heart is your Divine life force—the very energy or vibration that keeps you alive. The Sacred Heart is within you right now, waiting to be awakened and acknowledged and grown. When you pass from this life, this life force, your Sacred Heart, goes to another plane. Your body dies but your Sacred Heart lives on forever and until we recognize that we have this Sacred Heart inside us, we'll never fully recover from the abuse. Only when we see, truly see, our greatness, our Divine Light within, will we be whole.

As we move towards being whole, we will come to consider ourselves holy. And eventually we'll see everyone else as holy. Every person has this Sacred Heart, this Divine Light, inside. Some are so far from knowing who they really are, that they act out in violence and brutality, striving to hurt others so as to not feel less than others. With our new-found acceptance of who we really are, we stop our behaviors that aren't really working anyhow. We come to see that we don't need to have the drugs and alcohol to smother our inner pain. Our eating habits change, our shopping habits change, and our relationships with others change. We begin to feel a peace inside, a feeling of being okay with ourselves and with the world. We stop measuring ourselves against everyone else, because now we know who we really are. We know we are divine children of God – not some throwaway piece of human flesh that is less than everyone else. We're all equally wonderful! We all have a Sacred Heart within! As renowned spiritual leader and physician Dr. Deepak Chopra states, "Once you know who you really are, being is enough. You feel neither superior to anyone nor inferior to anyone and you have no need for approval because you've awakened to your own infinite worth."

The next three chapters are about healing each of the circles of the Sacred Heart—the Mind, the Body and the Spirit. I'll explain various activities that I've done to help me heal each segment of the Sacred Heart and show you how I've had to change my thinking to further restore my Spirit. These three areas, Mind, Body and Spirit, obviously overlap and are interconnected to form the Sacred Heart, so an activity or affirmation that I may suggest for healing the Body will also be therapeutic to the Mind and Spirit, as well. I've tried to describe what worked best for me and what area of my Sacred Heart seemed to benefit the most from certain methods. My division of these three elements in this section is simply my attempt at organizing the various spiritual activities and practices that have been beneficial to me. Any one of these methods may help heal the mind and the body and the spirit, but sometimes, it felt like a particular practice helped me more strongly in one area than the others. If so, I included it in that area.

Your experience will ultimately be different than mine, but I feel that we all should know how to heal the whole person—the Mind, the Body and the Spirit—and allow the Sacred Heart to shine. You may choose to work on your Spirit area first, and then move slowly into the Body and Mind. Others will feel drawn to explore the Body element first. It doesn't really matter what order you apply or try these new ways of healing. It doesn't matter if you try one of my suggestions and it doesn't work for you. Try something else. My hope is to have you learn some new activity or way of thinking that will lead you closer to feeling more peace within and to having you regain the power of your Sacred Heart.

Healing the Mind

Self Talk & Meditation

THERE'S A LITTLE PERSON INSIDE your head that never shuts up. She yaps her bloody mouth all the time and most of what she says is harsh and nasty. She belittles you, berates you, limits you and denies you. She's bitchy and superior and says she knows what's best for you. She makes you feel lousy, fat, unlovable, and she's got you right where she wants you. You believe her! She controls your emotions and controls your behavior. But, it's time to make her sit down and shut up!

But you can't make her stop until you really listen to her. Before I started my therapy, I didn't even know she existed. I listened to that voice in my head and thought it was all true! I believed the criticism and self-doubt. I let her berate me and I would feel so terrible inside. I would feel so unwanted and would feel so alone.

It was crucially important to find out what phrases, sayings, thoughts and beliefs she was parading around in my mind. Most of us are oblivious as to how we talk to ourselves every minute of the day, but our low self-worth is evident in the way we disapprove of ourselves. We deny ourselves the pleasures in life. We stop ourselves from exploring new venues. We criticize ourselves and put ourselves down in ways that cut us to the quick. We don't allow ourselves to enjoy our bodies sexually in a loving relationship. We don't try new things because we just know we'll fail. We know our weaknesses and we beat ourselves up about them.

We must start to listen and write down the messages this little brat is saying in our heads. We must pay attention to those automatic tapes running in our minds. We can't change any of her messages until we become aware of them. Once you become aware of what she is saying, you then can change the message. This is what Louise Hay calls "The Point of Power." In her wonderful book, *You Can Heal Your Life*, she states:

> The Point of Power is always in the present moments. You are never stuck. This is where the changes take place, right here and right now in our own minds! It doesn't matter how long we've had a negative pattern or an illness or a poor relationship or lack of finances or self-hatred. We can begin to make a shift today.

Louise goes on to say, *"You are the only person who thinks in your mind! You are the power and authority in your world!"*

Once you become aware of what she (the brat) is saying in your head, you can replace the negative, limiting lines with more positive, uplifting messages. Because of our abuse, we have internalized the negative, damaging energy from our abuser (and anyone else) and believe that's who we are! We have continued to abuse ourselves and create more dents by the persistent negative chatter that goes on in our heads.

I learned part of this method of changing my thoughts during sessions with my therapists. It's called Cognitive Behavioral Therapy (CBT) and attempts to correct ingrained patterns of negative thoughts and behaviors. It's wonderfully successful! But what I learned in my therapy sessions only took me so far. The things I've learned during my spiritual quest have helped extend the benefits of CBT. I not only stopped the negative thinking, I replaced those false beliefs with wonderful, life-affirming options.

You can apply this to almost any situation. I often used this same technique when I taught basic mathematics at a local college to adults who were returning back to school. They were always so afraid of taking a math class after being out of school for years. On the first day of class, I would ask them to tell me what messages they were hearing in their heads. I would hear the same things every semester:

- I'll never pass this class.
- I can't do fractions (or percentages or algebra or whatever)
- I couldn't do math in high school. I'll never be able to learn it now.
- It's been 15 (or 20 or 30) years since I've been in school. I've forgotten all my math.
- I'm afraid of embarrassing myself.
- My third grade teacher said I was terrible at math.
- My Mom said that none of the women in our family can do math.
- I'm going to fail all my tests.
- I'm too old to learn.

I had them write all of these down and we would add to the list throughout the semester. We would occasionally discuss how their self-talk was changing throughout the semester and they often would bring up a new phrase or self-criticism they heard while studying. The first step to changing your self-talk is to become aware of it.

The second step is to replace a negative word or phrase with something more positive. So, on that first day of class, we developed a list of encouraging phrases that they could use when hearing a negative sentence in their head. If someone heard herself say in her head, "I'm too old to learn," she would replace it with "I learn everything with ease." When they heard "I'll never be able to divide decimals," they replaced it with "I'm able to learn math easily now." When they heard the 3rd grade teacher shriek "You'll never be good at math," they now replaced it with "I'll learn my math lessons, one day at a time."

We had fun with it! A laid-off steel worker would come into class beaming, saying "Guess what I heard in my head last night?" and then surprise us with a terribly negative phrase his Dad told him about his abilities when he was seven. Folks would also create their own positive statements that meant something very personal to them and they would proudly read them out loud to the class. Before we would take a test, I would ask them what messages were floating around in their brains. We might repeat the phrase "I can pass this math test with a good grade." If they got stuck on a math problem during the test and felt themselves start to panic, they knew to put their pencils down, take 3 deep breaths and say to themselves, "I can do this. Jeanne taught me how math works." We made it a partnership between us. They weren't doing this alone. I would often write a positive statement on the board while they were taking a test, that they could glance up at. I also would have them write "I can pass this test with ease!" on the top of their test paper, so that they could read it throughout the test-taking process.

We brought their fears out into the daylight and watched them disappear. As we discussed their insecurities, we found out they just weren't true. They were belief systems they had bought into at an early age, but they had never been re-examined with a critical eye to see if they were true. And as they looked at these negative messages, they realized they really weren't true.

So the same is true for us victims of sexual abuse. We bought into the beliefs of our abusers. We believed our parents and our teachers. We were told things that just weren't true and we believed them. This creates our belief system and as Don Miguel Ruiz states in his powerful little book, *The Four Agreements*, "..we need a great deal of courage to challenge our own beliefs." We have the power within to change those beliefs.

Here are some of the hurtful things that my Dad said to me:

- Nobody will ever want you now.
- You're so ugly.

- What an ugly body you have.
- You're used goods now.
- You won't amount to anything.
- You drive okay, for a girl.

So now, when I hear one of these phrases surface in my head, I simply say "Cancel that. I have a beautiful, healthy body." Or sometimes I'll visualize myself erasing the harmful statement from a whiteboard and envision a new sentence that says "I am lovable." The key point is to become aware of the thoughts in your head and take control of them. Your ego, or personality, will try and control the real you by using these limiting, damaging thought forms. Once you become aware of these negative thoughts and beliefs, you can change them to kinder, more life-affirming statements that will benefit your mind, body and spirit.

One of the most powerful things you can do is to look yourself in the eye in a mirror everyday and say "I love you." You may not even be able to do this at all at first, so start with just saying "I love you" silently, with no mirror involved. Then eventually say "I love you" out loud. Work your way up to saying "I love you" out loud while looking in your own eyes. Be prepared for an inner jolt and some warm tears.

I've compiled a list of affirmations for you. Some I've borrowed from Louise Hay's *You Can Heal Your Life* and Wayne Dyer's *The Power of Intention*, while some of them are my own. I've organized them into categories and started each one with an example of a negative thought form. Then there are several more positive statements that can be used to replace the negative thought. I've found for myself that when I'm feeling depressed it's very difficult to think of positive replacements on my own, so having some suggestions handy really helped me. The examples I found in various books helped prompt me into new ways of thinking. Use these as they are or meld them into something that feels more personal to you. Listen to your gut. What does it tell you? What do you need to hear to become well? There's a blank space in each category where you can write in your own positive affirmation.

Affirmations

Healing the Body	
Negative:	I have (disease). I hurt, ache, etc. I'm going blind, bald, deaf, etc. I can't walk, write, bend, see, etc.
Replace with:	I am healthy, whole and complete.
	I listen with love to my body's messages.
	I forgive _____.
	My body is restored to perfect health.
Change	
Negative:	I hate change!
Replace with:	I accept change with ease.
	I am in the rhythm and flow of ever-changing life.
	I see my patterns and I choose to make changes.
	When I change the way I look at things, the things I look at change.
	I am willing to change.
Finances	
Negative:	My finances are a mess. I'll never get out of debt. I don't have enough money.
Replace with:	The abundance of the Universe is available to everyone.
	I am a magnet for Divine prosperity.
	I attract success and abundance into my life because that is who I am.

Success	
Negative:	I just can't win! This isn't going to work.
Replace with:	Everything I touch is a success.
	I move into the Winning Circle.
Employment	
Negative:	I hate my job! I'll never find a job!
Replace with:	I am open to new employment opportunities.
	I always work for wonderful supervisors.
Relationships	
Negative:	Nobody loves me. I'm so lonely. I'll never get married. I hate my family.
Replace with:	All of my relationships are harmonious, warm and loving.
	I have a wonderful, new partner.
	I belong.
	It is my intention to be authentic and peaceful with all my relatives.
General	
Negative:	My life is a mess.
Replace with:	All is well.
	Everything is working in Divine order for my highest good.
	I am willing to release the need for these negative patterns in my life.

	The past has no power over me.
	I am willing to release the pattern within me that is creating this condition.

Weight Gain

Negative:	I'm so fat!
Replace with:	My body is healthy and slender.
	I intend to be at my perfect weight.
	Say "I love you" to your inner child.

Residence

Negative:	I want to move.
Replace with:	I have the perfect living space.
	The cutest apartment is coming to me now.

Self Worth

Negative:	I'm not good enough.
Replace with:	I deserve the best, and accept it now.
	I love and approve of myself.
	I am whole and perfect as I was created.
	I am a beautiful pearl of God.
	I am willing to release the need to be unworthy. I am worthy of the very best in life, and I now lovingly allow myself to accept it.

Sadness/Depression	
Negative:	It's no use. I'll never be happy.
Replace with:	I am joyous, happy and free.
	I have a purpose here on Earth.
	I want to feel good!
	I am a spiritual being inside. That being is perfect and unharmed.
Chaos and Disorder	
Negative:	I can't take all this drama! Everything's a mess!
Replace with:	I attract only peace in my life.
	I intend to live a stress-free and tranquil life.
	I release this old idea and let it go.
Learning / Education	
Negative:	I'm not smart enough. I'm too old to learn.
Replace with:	I learn new ideas very easily.
	I am open to new wisdom and knowledge.
Forgiveness	
Negative:	I hate him! I'm so angry at her for what she did! You betrayed me! I'll never forgive him!

Replace with:	I release the past and forgive everyone (or replace with a specific name).
	I forgive you for not being the way I wanted you to be.
	I forgive you and I set you free.
	I set down my anger and release myself from this whirlwind of resentment. I forgive you.
	I let go and let God.
Sex	
Negative:	Don't touch me. Sex is dirty. It's the only thing men think about. If I have sex with him, then maybe he'll love me.
Replace with:	I love my body and want to share it with another within a healthy relationship.
	Sex is a beautiful, loving act between two people.
Fear	
Negative:	The world is not a safe place to be. Don't trust anyone.
Replace with:	I am safe now.
	Nothing will harm me again.
	There is a bubble of God's love surrounding me wherever I go.

I Painted the Light

On page 164 of Wayne Dyer's wonderful book, *The Power of Intention*, he writes that "What you think about expands." This is one of the laws of the universe. Whatever you give your attention to will grow. When you think negative thoughts and dwell in fear and anger, you attract people and events that will bring you more of the same. That energy level or vibration attracts more negativity, fear and anger. The chaos continues and grows.

But the good news is that we have the power to stop the chaos and negative flow of our life by changing the way we think. At every moment, we have power. We can change the direction of our thought patterns at any time and redirect the course that our life is taking. Own your power. Take control of your old patterns of negative thinking and gently, slowly replace the lower vibrational thoughts with higher vibrational thoughts and your life will change. Like a magnet, you'll start attracting better people and events into your life. You'll be more in alignment with Spirit and the good will flow to you. Wayne Dyer further states in his book on Page 166 that:

> By putting your attention on what you intend to manifest rather than on the same low energy that you encounter, you make a decision to connect to intention and bring the attributes of your universal Source to the presence of that low energy.

Gary Zukav wrote a fabulous book called *The Seat of the Soul* about the struggle between our soul and our personality. The personality holds onto our feelings and thoughts like shame, resentments and anger as a way of controlling us. By allowing our inner Light to step forward and be in charge, we can allow the healing process to unfold. He states on page 105-106:

> Energy continually pours through you, entering at the top of your head and descending downward through your body. You are not a static system. You are a dynamic being of Light that at each moment informs

the energy that flows through you. You do this with each thought, with each intention.

The Light that flows through your system is Universal energy. It is the Light of the Universe. You give that Light form. What you feel, what you think, how you behave, what you value and how you live your life reflect the way that you are shaping the Light that is flowing through you.

You change the way that you shape the Light which is flowing through you by changing your consciousness, by changing your thoughts. You do this, for example, when you challenge a negative pattern, such as anger, and consciously choose to understand and appreciate the needs of others. This creates different forms of thought, feeling and action. It changes your experience.

With each tiny thought that you change, you advance towards peace. With every sentence you say aloud, you have the power to choose where your energy is going. With every thought in your head you can continue to move downward towards lower frequencies by continuing your negative thinking or advance upwards towards higher vibrations and higher consciousness with uplifting and hopeful thoughts. Your Spirit will help you on this journey of healing. Take back your power. Shape your thoughts and your life will change. Shape your Light into a fully whole and peaceful human being.

MEDITATION

Sexual trauma has long-lasting negative effects on our physical, emotional, mental and spiritual bodies. It's a sucker-punch to every facet of our being. What we want most in life is to put everything back in working order. We want balance and harmony in our lives. We want a feeling of peace. Within our physical bodies, we want to relieve the pain we feel in our muscles, alleviate the headaches, lower our shoulders, and unclench our jaws. Mentally we want to stop the negative chatter, feel good about ourselves, and feel hope about our futures. We want to heal the deep emotional wounds of unworthiness, fear and anger. We want to nurture our spiritual essence and feel the joy of being one of God's creations. In other words, we want to be happy and at peace. We don't just want to survive, we want to thrive!

Meditation will help you with all four of these areas. It can alleviate the symptoms of post traumatic stress disorder, improve learning, and deepen your spirituality. If there is but one change to your lifestyle that you make from reading this book, I hope that it is adding a meditation practice to your daily routine. Meditation is easy, free and can be done anywhere by anybody. It has magnificent benefits for your mind, body and spirit.

When I first heard of meditation, I would think of gurus sitting cross-legged for hours, even days, in loin cloths in India or Nepal. There are those special spiritual leaders who practice in this fashion, but I'm talking about adding 10-20 minutes of peace into your everyday life. I'd like to share with you some ideas about what mediation is and isn't, explain how to meditate, give you the benefits of meditating and share some resources for you to learn more about the practice of meditation.

What It Is and Isn't

Meditation is a personal practice of tuning into your true essence. It's a method of training your concentration and focus to help you expand your spiritual awareness. Meditation is being used to help alleviate the symptoms of post traumatic stress disorder in schools, prisons, drug abuse rehabilitation centers, Indian reservations, homeless shelters and in homes just like yours. I use meditation to quiet my brain, rest my body and commune with God. There's a wonderful feeling of connectedness that I feel when I meditate. I can also feel the true qualities of my spirit, such as compassion, patience, and peacefulness, emerge when meditating.

Meditation is not of the occult. Meditation is not of the devil. It is not mind control by another person or being. It is a tool used for returning your body's chemical and physical functions to normal operating levels. It's a method for hushing the thoughts for awhile and allowing your soul to experience growth and relaxation.

Studies have been conducted showing the difference stages of brain function during meditation. The electroencephalogram (EEG) is the depiction of the electrical activity occurring at the surface of the brain. This activity appears on the screen of the EEG machine as waveforms of varying frequency and amplitude measured in voltage (specifically microvoltages).

EEG waveforms are generally classified according to their frequency, amplitude, and shape, as well as the sites on the scalp at which they are recorded. The most familiar classification uses EEG waveform frequencies: Beta Waves, Alpha waves, Theta waves, and Delta waves.

The EEG Brain Frequency Chart below shows the normal brain waves as people experience various states of alertness, creativity, and sleep.

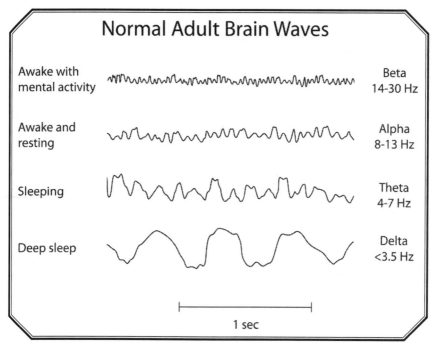

Brain Waves.

Beta waves   14–30 Hz—This is the frequency range for normal brain activity and ordinary consciousness. This range of brain waves occurs when we are riding our bike, balancing our checkbook or thinking about what plans to make for the weekend. It is also the vibration of our brain waves when we are experiencing strong negative emotions. This is the 'monkey brain' or brat that chatters to us about our faults and keeps us locked in negative self-talk.

Alpha waves   8–13 Hz—This is the frequency range of our brain when we are experiencing heightened awareness and calmness. Alpha waves are attained during light meditation and are present when we daydream. Research has shown that "superlearning" takes place in this state of awareness.

Theta waves   4–7 Hz—This is the frequency range of our brain waves when we are in a deep meditative state and during heightened states of creativity. In this state, we can access unconscious material, reveal insights and creative ideas. You may experience drowsiness in this level, and also the first stage of sleep.

Delta waves   1–3.5 Hz—This is the frequency range of our brain waves when we are in a deep sleep or a deep state of consciousness as from deep meditation.

As you meditate, you slow down the brain waves from Beta to Alpha and allow yourself to be alert but calm. Anxiety eases in this state. As you progress into your meditation, your brain waves reach the Theta state where your brain is highly creative and very relaxed. The Delta state is a very deep stage of meditation and gives your body and mind a "power nap."

Another interesting fact is that Mother Earth has her own

natural frequency of 7.8 hz. A person in a meditative state has a natural frequency of approximately 7.8 hz, as well. This is called the Schumann Resonating Frequency. The more time that we can spend in meditation and in nature, the more our own frequency will return to it's natural state—a level of awareness that offers us the best creativity, learning and calmness.

Meditation is Easy

Dr. Oz is a big proponent of mediation. On his website he has an article called "Less Stress With Meditation: 3 Easy Steps." Let me share a small part of that article here:

> Everybody wants a long life full of vitality. But beyond the basics of good diet and exercise, what can you do? For more than 2,000 years, Chinese medicine has refined the use of meditation to build the body's life force. And the scientists agree. The well-documented effects of regular meditation include lowered blood pressure, less heart disease, decreased chronic pain, and increased mental clarity. Meditation is an indispensable tool for living a longer, richer life and avoiding the burnout that comes from constant stress.

How to Meditate in 3 Steps

Many people find the idea of meditation to be daunting. They think they do not have the time, saying, "Someday I will devote the time to study meditation." Meditation is simple. You don't need training and you don't need to be alone in the mountains. All you need is a quiet place to sit and the curiosity to try for 10 minutes.

Step 1: Sit comfortably in a chair with your spine erect and both legs and thighs forming a ninety-degree angle with the ground, keeping your feet shoulder width apart—or sit in a cross-legged position.

Step 2: Close your eyes and breathe as naturally as possible. After a few breaths, try breathing with your abdomen only. Slowly, your breath will deepen as you practice.

Step 3: Begin to quiet your mind. Of course, the thoughts will come—and they will always be there. Don't struggle against them. Let the thoughts come, but don't dwell on them. Keep relaxing, and bring your consciousness back to your breath. If you have trouble concentrating, focus on one thing, a word or a mantra that can invoke a calming effect within you.

BENEFITS OF MEDITATION

Meditation provides unparalleled benefits to all of the major categories of human existence: Physical, Mental, Emotional and Spiritual. I've combined information from various websites about the specific benefits of meditation and the clinical studies that back these claims. These websites are listed at the end of this section. Let's take a look at how meditation can help you with the healing process.

Physical Benefits: Victims of sexual abuse often suffer from tense muscles, shallow breathing, headaches, fibromyalgia and other physical ailments. Meditation helps because it actually affects the chemistry and physiology of your cells. Through deep-breathing, which is the backbone of any meditation practice, muscle fatigue and tension are reduced by increasing the circulation of oxygen to the muscles. Meditation has also been proven to normalize blood pressure and reduce cholesterol due to its stress-reducing benefits. Meditation also helps to strengthen the immune system, as well. It induces the relaxation response which reduces the occurrence of pain, insomnia and migraines. Blue Cross/Blue Shield, a major health insurance provider, claims that those who practice Transcendental Meditation have 50% less medical claims than those who do not meditate. Another major physical benefit of meditation is unlimited energy. Meditation helps you to create an eternal and infinite flow of pure life-force energy. It has also been used to assist people with losing weight. Personally, meditation has helped me relax tight muscles, decrease my headaches and feel more at ease in my body. I feel less anxiety and experience more serenity in my daily experience. It brings a feeling of vitality and contentment to my life.

Emotional Benefits: Those of us who have been sexually abused often suffer from a heightened sense of alarm. Nothing feels safe anymore and we often stay in a mode of "fight or flight" response. This brings about irritability and inappropriate emotional responses. With meditation, I found a huge reduction in the "fight or flight" response and more emotional self-control. It helped me bring perspective when confronted with a crisis, thus making the situation more manageable. Managing our modern daily lives can become quite overwhelming when you factor in traffic jams, work related stress, toxicity overload and seemingly unmanageable schedules. Taking a small amount of daily time to meditate can bring the perspective you need to manage your busy schedule and bring back a feeling of "I can handle this." It helped lift the anger inside me.

Meditation will allow your senses to be heightened and aroused even during routine tasks, making your day more enjoyable. I started enjoying the subtleties of life again like the smell of fresh laundry or the taste of a clementine or the color of the morning sky. Learning to integrate all the senses in your daily life, through meditation, will bring a myriad of emotional benefits and fullness to your life and help you become a better observer. By being a better observer you can respond to situations rather than react, meaning you can act appropriately when you feel inspired or compelled to and in perfect timing.

With lower anxiety levels, I also started sleeping better which in turns brings better physical, mental and emotional benefits. Meditation helps reduce depression and diminishes violent outbursts. Studies have shown that meditation brings a greater sense of self-confidence and an increased outpouring of kindness and compassion. It brings us back to who we really are: Spiritual beings practicing loving kindness.

Mental Benefits: Sexual abuse often leaves us with edgy nerves, a chattering mind, achy shoulders and sleepless nights. This all leads to lower brain functioning and poor memory recall. Meditation can help bring better mental focus, improved concentration and increased creativity into your life. It reduces the stress and anxiety we're feeling and brings us greater peace of mind. Meditation seeks to bring harmful and counter-productive thoughts and feelings to the surface within you, quell them and help you gain the necessary perspective to invoke more truth and reality in your life. Studies about meditation have shown wonderful improvements in both short-term and long-term memory, along with the ability to raise your IQ, at any age! Persistent stress can stop some brain functions, but meditation can actually heal the brain waves and make them perform to their optimum ability. The mental benefits of meditation, if regularly practiced, are long lasting and eventually become permanent.

RESOURCES

There are thousands of websites that exist with free meditations. You can do further reading about the benefits of meditation, search for different methods, listen to music that feeds your soul, or find a mantra that feels right for you. Search for groups in your area that meditate together and possibly take a class in meditation. Watch YouTube videos to explore various modes of meditation. Find what is comfortable for you. And practice. Every day.

I've listed just a few sites below that will help you get started on your meditation journey:

- Dr. Deepak Chopra, www.chopra.com
- Dr. Wayne Dyer , www.drwaynedyer.com
- The David Lynch Foundation, www.davidlynchfoundation.org
- The Mayo Clinic, http://www.mayoclinic.com/health/meditation/HQ01070
- National Ctr for Complementary & Alternative Medicine, http://nccam.nih.gov/health/meditation
- The Transcendental Meditation Program, http://www.tm.org/
- Dr. Oz, www.doctoroz.com

Healing the Body

Our beautiful bodies were violated and used for selfish reasons by our abusers. Our tender physical vessels that provide a home for our gentle Spirits were subjected to assault and attack that was sometimes vicious and cruel. We may have broken bones from being forced to submit, torn vaginal walls from the rapes, scars from knife wounds and other physical evidence of the brutal attacks. The bruises have faded but there may be other signs on your body that remind you of your past trauma.

I was made to perform oral sex on my father countless times during my childhood. Keeping my mouth held open for long periods of time eventually tore the discs between my skull and jaw bone (mandible). In my twenties, I had terrible, debilitating headaches and was eventually diagnosed with TMJ—Temporal Mandibular Joint dysfunction. I had bilateral jaw surgery where the surgeon made incisions behind my ears and folded my ears forward onto my face. He was able to retrieve the misplaced discs, which were lying in the bottom of my jaw, patch the holes in them with skin grafts from my thigh, and sew them back into place in the joint in front of the ears. The headaches vanished for the most part, but I still have them when I get tense and clench my teeth. I also have problems going to the dentist and holding my mouth open for extended periods of time. My dentist and hygienist are aware of my background and know to give me frequent breaks when I'm having dental work done. The sexual abuse may leave lasting physical evidence on our bodies.

But sexual abuse can also leave its mark in the very cells of our bodies. Cellular memory holds the feelings of fear and terror within our muscle tissues causing our bodies to feel tired, achy and tense. These are common symptoms of Post Traumatic Stress Disorder (PTSD) felt by sexual abuse victims, war veterans or any type of trauma survivors. Our bodies' cells remember our stories, even when our brain has repressed the memories. One of my favorite books, *The Courage to Heal*, a best-selling guide for sexual abuse survivors, has the slogan, "The body remembers what the mind forgets."

Some of the physical damage done to your body may never be healed. You may always have the scars of the knife wound or cigarette burns. I may always have a slight feeling of achiness in my jaw and a limited range of motion with my mouth. That I can live with. But what I wanted to heal was the general anxiety and stress I felt throughout my body. I wanted to be able to relax. I wanted to feel comfortable in my own skin. This is an area that I still work on, but I've found several methods that have been beneficial to me.

THE POWER OF WORDS

Did you know that every word has a vibration? Your spoken words, your written words and your unspoken words in your mind all have a vibrational frequency that affects the environment, including your physical body. They especially impact the quality and life force of the water you drink. Dr. Masuru Emoto of Japan has done extensive research into the power of words and has published several books including *Miraculous Messages from Water, How Water Reflects our Consciousness*.

In his experiments, Dr. Emoto would tape various words, such as "Love and Gratitude" or "You Fool," to bottles of ordinary tap water. He would then freeze the water and photograph the ice crystals as they formed. The results were amazing! The crystals from the "Love and Gratitude" bottle were beautiful, detailed ice formations, while the photos taken of the "You Fool" water were dark and distorted with no sign of crystal formations at all. As you observe these two photos, think about the profound effect that words have on water.

Love and Gratitude

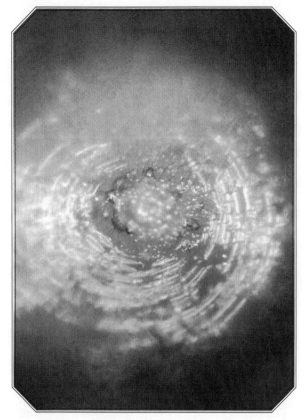

You Fool

He also tested the effect of prayer on water. By taking photos of the crystals from water before and after prayers were administered, he was able to show how our thoughts and words affect the very structure of the water itself. The pictures below display the crystals made from water from the Fujiwara Dam before and after Buddhist prayers were offered to the water.

I Painted the Light

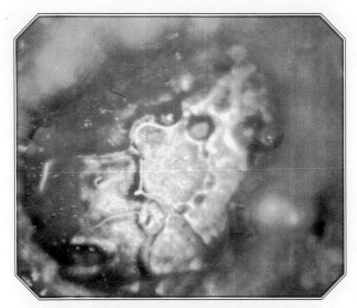

Before Buddhist prayers

After Buddhist prayers

Dr. Emoto also experimented with pictures and found there were similar results. He would paste a picture onto the side of a bottle of water or set the bottle on a photograph for a period of time and then freeze the water. For example, he sat a bottle of water atop a picture of Mother Teresa and another bottle of water atop a picture of Adolf Hitler. The results were amazing! Major differences were seen between the crystals from these two bottles of water. The beautiful, detailed crystal created by the water sitting on Mother Teresa's photo was in sharp contrast to the murky blobs that came from the water sitting on Adolf Hitler's picture. The water could 'feel' the energy of these people.

The point here is if our thoughts and words, both spoken and written, affect the molecular structure of water, and if our bodies are approximately 70% water, what effect are our thoughts and words having on our bodies? What effect is the music that you're listening to having on your body? What types of words are your friends and family saying to you? Are they supportive or damaging? Changing the words you use in your own conversations and in your thoughts can literally change the molecular structure of your body. Changing the type of music you listen to and the type of movies you watch will affect the health of your body on a cellular level. Do you need to set boundaries with people and limit the harmful words they say to you? Do you need to find new friends?

Be careful of the words you think and the words you say. Be careful what music, movies and conversations are in your environment. Your body is listening and responding. The vibrational energy of words and sounds has an impact on your physical health.

Learn more about Dr. Emoto's fascinating work at www.masaru-emoto.net or www.whatthebleep.com/crystals. You can also search Amazon and YouTube for examples of his work.

Music & Sound Healing

Music has played an important part in my recovery from sexual abuse. The agitated, nervous feelings inside me could be often soothed with the lift of a voice or the sweet melody of harmonies played on wonderful instruments. I found many of the New Age artists I love simply by accident. I would go into the local Border's Book & Music store, put on a pair of the available headphones and listen to the wonderful songs created by these contemporary artists. These were not songs found on the local radio stations so there was no name recognition of the musicians or song titles. It was simply by listening and closing my eyes that I found the music that spoke to my soul. Sometimes a Celtic run would be pleasing and sometimes I found the same song abrasive. I longed for something deeper than could be spoken with words. I needed something to heal the brokenness inside, to smooth out the jagged edges of my nerves and to curb my fears of going insane. Music was an important step in holding me steady and making me whole.

Often I would find the brash announcers of the radio stations and the loud advertisements from annoying car dealers (why do they always scream?), an intrusion into my already chaotic world. Likewise, television was crowded with terribly negative news stories and inane programming. I craved something softer and more comforting than my world already was, not additional noise and chaos. I needed something I could escape into, something that would let me feel the harmonies inside me. I wanted something that would allow me to run away from the stress of the day, the technical difficulties I had encountered, and the endless stream of disagreeable messages in my head. I kept myself surrounded by a few reliable CDs that I could pop into my car stereo or my CD player at home that could steady the jangled and confused areas of my psyche. I could feel my shoulders lower as I listened to a melodic tune with harps and violins or acoustic guitars and harmoniums.

I started listening to the CD *White Stones* by Secret Garden and just about anything from Steve Halpern. The music created by Windham Hill was as good as a nerve pill and with no side effects. The Celtic soloist, Enya, could help me float away on her beautiful voice, as could the delightful sounds of Sarah McLaughlin.

We have known for ages the power of music. We sing soft

lullabies to our babies and energize the football crowd with the heightened sounds of brass and percussion of the high school band. A Sousa march will make us feel like we're part of the parade! When we want to create a sexy environment, we put on some Barry White or some soft jazz tunes. For parties, I can't wait to return to the songs of my earlier years played by Aerosmith, The Beatles, The Rolling Stones, The Doobie Brothers or Santana. And no island party would be complete without a Jimmy Buffett sing-a-long or reggae beat from Bob Marley. We use music to create the mood. We send certain vibrations into the air to create an environment conducive to relaxing, dancing, cheering or making love. I used music to heal and I want you to experience the same healing effects of music.

There's science now to back up the claims of sound healing. Research is now proving that we can send vibrations into ourselves to create a healing space within. Don Campbell's wonderful book, *The Mozart Effect, Tapping the Power of Music to Heal the Body, Strengthen the Mind, and Unlock the Creative Spirit* has shown us the incredible power of music on our damaged bodies and psyches. As stated in his book, Campbell lists that music:

- Masks unpleasant sounds and feelings
- Slows down and equalizes brain waves
- Affects respiration
- Affects heartbeat, pulse rate, and blood pressure
- Reduces muscle tension
- Improves body movement and coordination
- Affects body temperature
- Increases endorphin levels
- Regulates stress-related hormones
- Boosts the immune function
- Changes our perception of space and time
- Strengthens memory and learning

- Boosts productivity
- Enhances romance and sexuality
- Stimulates digestion
- Fosters endurance
- Enhances unconscious receptivity to symbolism
- Generates a sense of safety and well-being

A main theme throughout his book is that so many of our bodily functions exist on the patterns of vibration. Our physical body has a natural rhythm, our mental state has a natural vibration, our emotional state has a normal frequency, and so on. When we're sexually abused, it's as if all our vibrational patterns are disturbed and out of sync, making us feel different and unsettled. We don't fit into our bodies well, and hence we don't fit into relationships and society well. Music can help change that. By finding the right music that speaks to you on an intuitive level, you can find the right pattern needed for correcting **your** out-of-sync systems.

Dr. Emoto also experimented with the effect of music on water. Heavy metal music or rap music with negative lyrics created formations that were distorted and dark. But water that listened to classical music or were exposed to John Lennon's song *Imagine* created stunning, light-filled crystals. You can view these photos in Dr. Emoto's books or visit his website, www.masaru-emoto.net.

Dr. Deepak Chopra explains in his book *Perfect Health* that there are "invisible threads" composed of faint vibrations that hold together our atoms, cells and tissues. An illness or accident, or maybe abuse, can alter this vibration making our bodies perform at less than optimal levels. This out-of-sync vibration can be recalibrated through the use of tones, chants, and music. From Campbell's book he states that:

> Practitioners of traditional Chinese medicine and philosophy agree, teaching that each cell in the body is the terminus of a tiny capillary and a meridian, bringing together blood, ki or life energy,

and consciousness. According to this vibrational model, sounds and images are received, archived, and transmitted not only through the brain, but also through other organic structures and functions. That means that, as a result of sickness, accident or *trauma*, painful emotions and experiences can become locked in the body, and can remain there for weeks, months, and even years until released—in many cases by the right sounds and images.

Jonathon Goldman is another expert in the field of Sound Healing. One of his basic principles of using sound to heal is that of resonant frequency healing. Every object and every body part has its own frequency or sound, even though we cannot hear it. Within the field of bio-resonance, modern science is verifying that each organ, bone and tissue resonates or vibrates at its own frequency. The heart has its own vibrational frequency, the liver has its own vibrational frequency, our skin has its own vibrational frequency. When a tissue's frequency has been altered due to an accident or trauma, it does not perform at its prime ability. By reestablishing the correct frequency upon a tissue, harmony returns and the body performs at its best. This process of **entrainment** "is a phenomenon of sound in which the powerful vibrations of one object will actually change the vibrations of another object, causing this second object to lock in step or synchronize with this first." (Goldman, online course). We are able to shift the frequency of a specific organ or our entire body to its normal level and thus be in sync with the energies surrounding it. When we create this subtle shift of vibration within ourselves, we aid in our healing. We bring our body back to its normal level where it can naturally heal and create harmony within itself.

From Goldman's course, I learned about Dr. Hans Jenny, a Swiss scientist who studied the effects of sound upon organic matter. He called the work **cymatics**—the study of waveform phenomena. Using various organic substances vibrated at different frequencies, he found repeatable patterns that represented cellular growth, mandalas, and microscopic life forms. From his work it has been proposed that sound creates form and changing frequencies affect form at a cellular level. Now, using laser technology, physicists are also finding that harmonic intervals produce perfect geometric shapes, reinforcing the idea that vibration underlies all form.

The music you listen to can assist you in your journey to wholeness. As you continue with your therapist, or after therapy has done its best, you can continue healing yourself through the continued use of toning, chants and music. You can use it on a daily basis as a way of centering yourself and bringing your consciousness to Light. The frenzied, chaotic whirlwind I often found inside myself could be tamed with the use of the right music, the right chant or the right tone. Inside I could feel the frazzled nerves calm down and play nice with each other! Music helps me release the blocked emotions that are stored inside the very cells of my body. The healing music creates an energy field full of possibility. Allow your physical body, your emotional body and your psychological body to reap the benefits of the healing tones of music. In Appendix 1, I have listed the talented musicians and the CDs I listened to for assistance in my healing. This list by no means shows the multitude of music that can be used for this purpose. Find the music that is right for you. Explore your local stores or listen online to the samples of artists. Let your gut tell you what your system needs. The music you need will change over time. As one area of you heals, another piece of music will call to you, as that is what is needed now. Share the oneness of love that these artists have created. Listen to these wonderful melodies for your pleasure and for your return to wholeness.

MANTRAS

A mantra is a word or sound used in a spiritual practice to connect with the Divine. I was taught in my childhood that mantras were not of God and so I considered them to be something associated with cults, weirdoes, or even the devil. My religious training taught me to fear these strange mutterings and the people involved with them. My white, middle-to-lower-class, Mid-West cultural surroundings limited my exposure to anything that was not conservative Americana. So I mistrusted people who spoke of mantras. I avoided them. But thankfully I was exposed to mantras, and the related chanting rituals, in safe surroundings from people I trusted and liked which allowed me to change my belief system about them. Mantras have significantly aided in my healing, and have happily broadened my world view.

A **mantra** is a sound, syllable, word, or group of words that is considered capable of "creating transformation." Wikipedia states that their use and type varies according to the school and philosophy associated with the mantra. Mantras originated in the Vedic tradition of India, later becoming an essential part of the Hindu tradition and a customary practice within Buddhism, Sikhism and Jainism. The use of mantras is now widespread throughout various spiritual movements which are based on, or off-shoots of, the practices in the earlier Eastern traditions and religions. Repetition of prayers for the holy rosary is the Christian version of a mantra. The rosary is similar to the Indian prayer beads (or mala), as it is a string of beads used to count the number of prayers, or mantras repeated.

Mantras are effective tools which aid in reprogramming or re-patterning the very vibratory structure of one's inner mental makeup. In English language usage, the term "mantra" has a negative meaning quite distinct from prayer —a meaning that carries derogatory connotation of "mindless, thoughtless repetition of a concept." But it's anything but thoughtless. It is a purposeful way to bring you closer to God and to your own feeling of the Divine within. Mantras can be extremely helpful in healing the effects of abuse. To utilize a mantra, find a quiet space, close your eyes and repeat the word or phrase to yourself, either out loud or quietly in your head, over and over again. Start with about 10 minutes a day. You may find that you start rocking or swaying as you repeat the sounds. Allow your body to do what it wants to do. It knows what it needs. The gentle motions are soothing and can add to the overall effect of your mantra.

One of the first mantra exercises I learned was the Buddhist phrase of 'Nam Myoho Renge Kyo.' In very brief terms, this mantra speaks about the Mystic Law representing both the seen and unseen aspects of life. It honors the Lotus Flower which represents the natural law of cause and effect and the connectedness of all. This phrase, Nam Myoho Renge Kyo, is usually spoken repetitively in either a slow or rapid cadence, or a combination of both. There's a great video on YouTube of Larry King and Tina Turner discussing her chanting practice of Nam Myoho Renge Kyo. Check it out to see how to say the words. Then try it out for yourself. Sit down in a quiet space, close your eyes and repeat the phrase, Nam Myoho Renge Kyo.

I also have a mantra given to me by my Transcendental Meditation teacher. I meditate in many ways, but when applying the TM style, I repeat my mantra silently over and over until I enter a state of oneness. When a thought enters my mind, I let it go, and start back with repeating my mantra. You can receive a mantra from a TM teacher, a guru, or you can choose a word or phrase that suits you.

The word "OM" is a great mantra. It's the Hindu word for peace. It's a primal sound representing the entire Universe. Its vibration is very high and can create significant changes in your vibrational frequency. At Merging Hearts Holistic Center, we end each Sunday morning session, called Enlightened Beings, with everyone standing in a circle holding hands and chanting "OM" three times together. It's a powerful practice that creates wonderful good vibrations both in the room and within each one of us.

Here again, science is showing that repeating mantras creates healing within our bodies and minds. Dr. Herbert Benson, M.D., of the Mind/Body Medical Institute at Boston's Deaconess Medical Center, having studied the effects of chanting mantras on human physiology, found that repeating a single syllable or word produced measurable changes in energy consumption, respiration rate, heartbeat, metabolic rate and pulse, as well as an increase in alpha brain waves. His book, *The Relaxation Response*, has helped millions of people cope with anxiety and stress.

Choosing a mantra is as simple as finding one that resonates with you. Instead of just a single word, you may want to choose a phrase for a mantra. Here are some examples:

- I am Love.
- Let there be peace.
- I live only in the present.
- Live and let live.
- I am safe in God's arms.
- I am surrounded by love.

Sometimes it helps that the words are in English and sometimes it's best when they are in Hindu or Sanskrit. My mind tends to hang on to the English words more which isn't necessarily good. When saying something like, "I am surrounded by love", my mind can then interject with a doubt or sarcastic quip like, "Yeah, right!" If the same phrase is spoken in another language, my higher self knows the meaning, but the thinking brain can't make sense of it and therefore can't deny it. Search your local area for a meditation center, a yoga studio or a Transcendental Meditation teacher. With practice, you'll find just the right words or sounds to use to elevate your vibration and speed your process towards inner peace.

CHANTING

Chanting was definitely a new concept for me. I had vaguely heard of various religions who used chanting within their services or individual practices, but I had never seen it in person or taken part in such an activity. From my limited world view, and as is typical of anything we see as different or unknown, I kind of feared it in a way. When I would see videos of folks chanting, they would almost appear to be in a trance and I saw it as a form of brain-washing or mind control. To summarize this practice, chanting is the rhythmic speaking or singing of words and/or sounds. Chants can range from the simple speaking of a phrase in a monotone style, a simple melody involving a limited set of notes, to highly complex musical structures. There is typically a great deal of repetition within the chant. This repetition at first seemed monotonous to me and without value, but I have found it serves two purposes for me. First, the repetition of the same words, phrases and notes keeps my mind (the monkey brain) busy doing something. I am then free to visit my internal world of Spirit. Secondly, the repeating notes and sounds allow my body and psyche to absorb the healing energy given off by these powerful words, phrases and tones. Words have energy attached to them. By chanting words that have a high vibration we create that same vibration in and around us.

Chanting is an ancient spiritual practice used in all parts of the world. Chanting is practiced within the African and Native American cultures. There are Gregorian chants, Vedic chants, Jewish liturgical music, Qur'an readings, Baha'i chants, Buddhist chants, and various Hindu mantras set to music. There are even chants found within the Roman Catholic, Eastern Orthodox, Lutheran and Anglican churches. (Wikipedia) The large mega-churches of today are using a form of chanting with their praise music. It's called "7-11" music. You repeat 7 words, 11 times. It's rhythmic and en-'chant'-ing!

A form of chanting that I enjoy is the musical, call-and-response style used in a traditional Kirtan. Kirtan is a Sanskrit word meaning "to repeat." I have the divine pleasure to have Kirtan artist, Craig (Narada) Wise, as my friend. He introduced me to this devotional style of chanting and has performed many wonderful Kirtans for The Merging Hearts Holistic Center on a regular basis. The Kirtan session involves the chanting of hymns or mantras to the accompaniment of instruments such as the harmonium, drums, acoustic guitar, and violin. Craig plays the harmonium and lovingly calls out the chant, while the rest of us respond by repeating the phrases or mantras back to him. The process becomes a beautiful dance between musician and participants. The magic starts to happen as you learn the Hindu phrases and can let go of your brain and sink into the movement of the tones and the rolling words of praise. The session leaves me feeling relaxed and filled with joy as my spirit swells with recognition of the Love of the Divine. I feel at one with all those in the room and with God. The energy we create together is thick and sweet. There is a healing quality to these Kirtans as I let go of "me" and merge with others as our spirits collectively fuse with the Divine. There are wonderful CDs available with Kirtan music. Play them at home and sing the responses back. Feel the vibrations inside as you resonate with the healing tones.

I also enjoy listening to Gregorian chants. These chants are a central tradition of Western Christianity and are often performed at Catholic Mass. The chants are also performed nine times a day by the monks living the monastic life. The music is sung without accompaniment and is comprised of simple melodies. The Benedictine Monks of Santo Domingo de Silos released their album, Chant, in 1994, and have sold over 5 million copies. I bought the CD some time after it came out because of all the publicity it was getting. I have to admit I listened to it maybe once or twice and then put it on the "what was all the excitement about" stack. It sat there for years until a friend advised me about using the Gregorian chants for healing purposes. I pulled it out and listened to it again. Now I was ready for it. There was something sacred that touched me—something genteel and comforting. I also received a message from my spirit guides to put on this Chant CD when writing this chapter. I feel like they are singing just for me as I receive divine assistance for my book. I have it playing right now as I write this, and the sweet vibrations that fill the room are graceful and nurturing. I would highly recommend playing this music after a hard day at work, when studying and when preparing to meditate. It's not just music, its prayer set into motion along the vocal cords of these pious lightworkers.

Dr. Andrew Weil, author, lecturer and founder of the Program in Integrative Medicine in Tucson, Arizona, is a big proponent of a new science called **psychoacoustics**—the study of the effect of music and sound on the human nervous system. Psychoacoustics shows that frequency can relieve pain, help stroke patients, and benefit other conditions." Allow music to help you on your road to recovery. Dr. Weil has created several CDs that blend the right combination of melodies, mantras and chanting to bring sound healing into your life.

According to author and lecturer Dr. Deepak Chopra, "The body is held together by sound, and the presence of disease indicates that some sounds are out of tune... primordial sound is the mysterious link that holds the universe together in a web that is the quantum field." Play the music, sing the songs, and speak the words that will bring your body's rhythms and vibrations back into harmony. The abuse has rattled your frequency cage. Healing music can help you clean house and restore balance to your physical body, your emotional well-being and your psychological state of mind.

While talking about vibrations and sound in relation to the human body, let's look at the chakra system and the various frequencies of each energy center. The chakra system is a Sanskrit concept referring to wheel-like vortices which, according to traditional Indian medicine, are believed to be the "force centers" of energy within the body. Seven major chakras or energy centers are generally believed to exist within the body and practitioners believe the chakras interact with the body's ductless endocrine glands and lymphatic system by feeding in good bio-energies and disposing of unwanted bio-energies. As we align our vibrations back into their normal frequencies, our physical, mental and emotional bodies heal and perform at their optimal levels.

Below is a picture showing the placement of the chakras within our bodies.

Chakra System

The chart shown below lists the placement in the body, the color, frequency, musical note and the healing attributes for each chakra.

Chakra System

Chakra	Placement	Color	Frequency	Note	Healing attributes
7th	Crown	Violet	960 hz	B	Spiritual Center; Psychic Abilities, Unity, Enlightenment
6th	Third Eye	Indigo	96 hz	A	Perception Center; Higher Consciousness, Intuition, Wisdom, Visualization, Aspiration for harmony.
5th	Throat	Blue	16 hz	G	Expression Center; Speak your Truth, Communication, Expression of Creativity (Arts/Music), Inner Voice
4th	Heart	Green	12 hz	F	Love Center; Forgiveness, Compassion, Unconditional Love, Hope
3rd	Solar Plexus	Yellow	10 hz	E	Power Center; Confidence, Self Esteem, Manifestation
2nd	Sacral	Orange	6 hz	D	Creativity and Sexual Energy Center; Ability to feel joy and pleasure
1st	Root	Red	4 hz	C	Survival and Security Center; Fear, Anger; Helps in Grounding, Dynamic,

As you can see, each chakra has its own unique frequency. In the chakra system, our chakra frequencies need to be balanced and properly resonating throughout the body. This is an important key to our overall physical, mental, emotional, and spiritual health. If they are balanced, we feel at peace and everything is working together in harmony. If a frequency is off balance, it throws our whole chakra system off. It's like listening to a radio that's not quite tuned in right. If we're not tuned into the right frequency, we get static. When we tweak the dial just a little, the noisy interference is gone and we have a clear signal. The same is true of our own electrical system. We have energy centers and meridians that run throughout our bodies. This system may be all haywire because of the abuse. We can have organs vibrating at rates that are not the norm and thus create dis-ease. Our nerves are shaky and our concentration is off. Music and sound are key elements to putting it all back in smooth, working order.

DRUMMING

Drumming is another way of healing using sound frequencies. The basis of using a drum head to create vibrations in the air follows the concept of entrainment. Drumming helps restore the synchronicity of the natural rhythms of our body and each of the various systems that work in conjunction with each other throughout our body. Much research has been completed on how drumming can facilitate healing within the physical and emotional body. Drumming has been used with Alzheimer patients, twelve-step programs and in hospital rehabilitation rooms. It helps fight depression, lowers hormone levels created by stress, increases the natural killer cell activity and enhances the immune system in cancer patients. For victims of sexual abuse it also helps us connect with our bodies again. So much of our conscious waking time is spent in a hyper-vigilant mode. We disown our bodies because we feel they have betrayed us or because they carry too much pain and memories.

Drumming helps me feel grounded. It helps me feel connected to other humans through a similar heartbeat and rhythm. Drumming feels earthy and primal and gives me a grand feeling of being connected to Mother Earth.

Join a drum circle!

Similar to meditation and any other form of sound healing, drumming facilitates changes in our brain. Drumming can take us from the beta wave state to the alpha wave state where connections can be made with higher consciousness, creative juices can be unleashed, and emotional and physical healing can take place.

When going to my first drum circles, I was self-conscious and was still holding on to my perfectionist attitude. I would barely pat the top of my drum in fear of making a mistake. I would look around the circle to see if anyone noticed what I was playing or if they noticed when I made a mistake (Really, there are no mistakes. It was just my perception that I was doing something wrong!). What

I noticed as I looked around the room was that no one was paying any attention to me. They were all lost in their own world of rhythm, pounding their drum in slow, repetitive beats or tapping away at a faster, higher-pitched rhythm. Some had their eyes open, while many others had their eyes closed and swayed to an internal beat. Others were bravely making their addition to the symphony as they sounded a cow bell or shook a gourd filled with dried seeds. These were noisy, not-to-be-ignored instruments and I thought I would never be good enough, or brave enough, to play these boisterous devices. And yet they added the spice to the overall sound that emitted from our circle. It took many, many drum circles before I could relax and become entranced by the sounds created by this wonderful community of people. It took many more drum circles before I could actually enjoy the sounds that I, myself, created and added to this wonderful community.

Drumming helped me in three important ways. First, drumming helped me experience my own significance, my own inner being, my own integral rhythm. I found a voice through my hands. I added to the complex nature of the group. I mattered.

Secondly, drumming helped me feel at one with all of humanity, connected within the wonderful mesh of human experience. Instead of feeling like the outsider, the one who is different like so many abuse victims feel, I felt a part of something bigger than myself. Again, I felt like I mattered. I felt like I belonged. I felt like I had something of importance to contribute to the complex web of rhythms surrounding me. The sense of belonging that comes with drumming is subtle, yet powerful. There are times when I don't want the drumming to end. I just want to continue with the blessed feeling of unity and community.

Thirdly, drumming helped me enter the spiritual realm. By losing myself in the rhythms and movement of the sound, I transcended the actual experience and entered an altered state of consciousness. I have often felt like I am floating about three feet above the floor during an intense drumming session. My Spirit is hovering in the mystical auric field outside my body. There's healing that takes place for the Mind, Body and Spirit when this altered state of awareness can be attained.

I eventually lost my fear of making mistakes and became braver with each drumming experience. I would try a new drum each round and listened intently at the way a rain stick would be added or how a wooden frog rasp was played. I don't have my own drum yet, but rely on the abundance of drums of my dear friends. But I feel that it won't be long before I purchase a drum of my own.

Drumming often inspires people to dance. The body seems to move effortlessly with the pulse of the solid bass drum or the syncopated rhythms of the faster beating drums. Dancing is another way of getting in touch with your body and feeling the beautiful flow of movement. Allow your body to let go of the tightness and rigid beliefs of right and wrong movement and allow it to flow in graceful, energetic motion. I experienced one drum circle in Asheville, NC where they hold a weekly drum circle in a park in the center of town. There were 40-50 drummers and just as many people dancing in the center. Some drummers held their drums on straps and both drummed and danced within the circle. I experienced their beautiful, positive energy and shared in their wonderful sense of community!

Look for a drum circle in your area. Check out the events by Jim Donovan or consider taking his workshop on how to facilitate a drum circle. You don't need to know how to play a drum to start a drum circle for your community. Let this talented musician, formerly the drummer with Rusted Root, show you how to bring rhythm, balance and fun into your life. I encourage counselors and others in service-oriented careers to take his class and incorporate the healing power of the drum into your practice. Check Jim out at www.JimDonovanDrums.com.

Other instruments, such as singing bowls and tuning forks, can also provide healing for our bodies. Like tuning a piano, your body can be tuned to achieve optimal physical balance. Utilizing singing bowls and tuning forks will instantaneously alter your body's biochemistry and bring your nervous system, muscle tone and organs into harmonic balance. I have worked only slightly with these methods of balancing frequencies, but would recommend them highly for continued sound healing.

Allow your mind, body and spirit to experience the healing power of sound. Be it music, chanting, mantras, drumming or tuning forks, let the frequencies of these various sounds soothe your thoughts, calm your body and lift your spirits. Search for Kirtans and drum circles on Google to find these healing pools of good vibes. Find those songs and chants that help you untangle the nerves and recover your normal frequency. Enlist the help of a skilled massotherapist who uses vibration in the form of singing bowls or tuning forks to bring your body into balance. Allow your intuition to find the "good vibrations" that will be healing for you.

And remember what Albert Einstein said, "Everything in life is vibration."

Body Work

Massage

Therapeutic massage is a wonderful way to alleviate the tension held in your body. Even a single session can lower your heart rate and make you feel more at ease. The increase in circulation brings a better flow of oxygen to your muscles which make them function better, plus it rids your body of harmful toxins. Massage helps lower your high blood pressure, improve your restricted breathing and strengthen your immune system.

Massage also helps release the harmful cellular memories that your body is holding onto. Soon after I started remembering my repressed memories, I had a massage with a wonderful woman named Peg. I was lying face up on the massage table in her beautiful therapy room. She was standing above my head and her gentle hands were massaging the back of my neck. It felt so good. I hold a lot of tension in my neck and shoulders, so it felt wonderful to feel the knots being gently worked out with her skilled fingers. She then cradled my head in her hands as her fingertips pushed on the pressure points at the base of my skull. Suddenly, a new memory of my father abusing me popped in my head. I started crying and telling her what was happening as the repressed memory surfaced. My left arm started jerking around and going into spasms. She told me to let it play itself out and not stuff it back inside again. I held my arm out from the side of my body perpendicular to the table and just let it jump about as I continued to sob on the table. She quietly guided me through the process of releasing that memory from my body. Peg wanted to hold me as I cried, but she didn't want to let go of the pressure points in the back of my head, so instead she softly laid her check on top of my forehead and stayed with me while I released this memory and the associated negative energy from my body. I was so scared. I was still new to having these repressed memories surface and I had never had my body go into these jerking movements before. Peg's kindness and sensitivity to my needs helped me through an emotional release during the massage. I have many friends who are massotherapists and they all have stories of major memory and energy releases while working with their clients. It may sound a bit scary, but with a kind and gentle massage therapist, you can unlock some of the stored negative energy you have in your body's cells and release them forever. I still have jerky movements in my arms and legs when I get a massage or when I'm meditating. Most of the time there are no new images or stories to go with the nervous twitches, but occasionally a buried memory will surface and I let it go. The body knows how to heal itself, if we give it the chance. When my arm or leg wants to jerk about in some form of spasm, I don't hold it back or try to cover it up. My body is trying to release some harmful energy pattern and I'm all for letting go of that!

Yoga

Any exercise program will help you relieve stress. Walking, weight lifting, biking, tai chi, and hiking are all wonderful ways to tone your body and release some of the cellular memory. Yoga is especially helpful because it is also realigning the chakra system and the flow of chi (energy/life force) throughout your body. With each stretch and pose, you'll feel yourself expanding and relaxing.

People who have suffered some type of trauma often have shallow breathing because of the anxiety they feel. Yoga will help you stretch the muscles around your shoulders and rib cage and open your air passages for deeper breaths. The breathing techniques taught in yoga classes will also help you learn how to breathe more deeply and fully. And the 10 minute rest/meditation at the end of a workout is simply heavenly. When I'm tense at work, I find that sometimes I'm actually holding my breath for long periods of time without even knowing it. I have a large magnet on my cabinet door that says "Breathe" in large, scripted letters. It always reminds me to take a minute to take several deep breaths and be in the moment before continuing on with my work. Find some type of exercise that you enjoy doing. You'll lose a few pounds and help your body in the recovery process from the sexual abuse. Yoga allowed me to start loving my body with kindness and tenderness.

Our bodies obviously took a lot of abuse while being exploited by our perpetrator. It's our job now to be gentle with ourselves. Find the right music to play to take the edge off a hard day. Sing a chant or repeat a mantra that will help change your body's vibrational level to a more harmonious plane. Join a drum circle and find your rhythm. Dance. Walk in nature or practice yoga to allow the cellular memory of the abuse to surface and escape, never to bother you again. Just like an onion, little by little, layer by layer, we peel away the layers of harm and neglect to reveal the beautiful child within. We reveal the beautiful Sacred Heart within.

Reiki

Reiki is another complementary health practice you could consider for healing your body. Reiki is an ancient Japanese technique used to promote healing in the body, reduce stress and encourage relaxation. It is administered by someone who has been attuned to the Reiki methods and uses a "laying on of hands" practice while the recipient stays fully clothed. It is based on the idea that an unseen life force energy (chi or ki) flows through us. The practitioner becomes a channel for this energy from Source to the patient. If one's life force energy is low, then we are more likely to get sick or feel stress, and if it is high, we are more capable of being happy and healthy. Reiki is a simple, non-invasive healing system that promotes health and well being and a wholeness of Mind, Body and Spirit.

I have been attuned in the Reiki tradition and both give and receive energy healings. I find them to be very therapeutic for myself and others. Explore the possibility of using this type of energy healing method for healing physical ailments and reducing stress. As you relax, your body triggers its own natural healing abilities for improved and sustained health.

Angel Ray Healings

Laura Lyn has been my friend for many years. I feel blessed to have her in my life. She has informed me through her wonderful Angel readings and has shared her unconditional love and guidance with me. When I was the President of The Merging Hearts Holistic Center in Canton, OH, I included Laura Lyn in our organization's schedule for many angel meditations and enlightening workshops, such as her Realm to Realm sessions. She has provided us with numerous fundraisers and has become an integral part of our organization's growth and well-being. We are truly fortunate to have her as a trusted friend and spiritual guide.

In addition to her Angel Readings and workshops, Laura Lyn offers healing work called Angel Ray Healings. They are offered as a set of three sessions and they are amazing. During these sessions, you lay on a massage table in a darkened room with incense and candles burning. There is wonderful angelic music filling the air. Laura Lyn starts each session with a prayer of protection and calls forth all the energies that will be for your highest good. She places stones and crystals at various points along your body, having standards for each of the chakra locations, but she also listens to her spirit guides for specific guidance as to what your body needs. She then calls in the various angels and their Healing Rays of Light to help heal your physical, emotional and psychological bodies. Archangels Michael, Uriel and Gabriel are invited into the room to shed their healing Rays of Light upon you. Other angels and spirit guides enter the room as well to lend their healing power to the session. Laura Lyn continues to pray for guidance and healing, and offers sincere gratitude to all those present. She may sing, chant, pray – whatever spirit moves her to do.

All of my Angel Ray Healing sessions were profoundly soothing. I felt both energized and calm. I was refreshed and a little light-headed on each of the occasions. Each was a beautiful experience and the calming effects lasted for several days after the session. But my most profound experience happened during my second session with her.

During my second visit, I was again laying on the table enjoying the lilting music and fragrant scents that filled the room. Laura had placed the sacred stones at their critical points along my body and I was relaxing as her soft voice enveloped me with her love. As Laura continued calling in the angels with their Healing Rays of Light, I suddenly felt something very strange happen. I suddenly felt myself sit up. I could feel something lift out of me. My spirit-self sat up, while my physical self was still lying on the table. With my eyes still closed, I could see in my mind's eye the back, the arms, and the back of the head of this being. I felt a little startled and thought, "What's going on?" And then this being turned and looked over her left shoulder. She continued to rotate her body and left arm around and eventually turned her head around enough to look me in the eyes!

She continued to gaze softly into my eyes and then she smiled! She smiled this gentle, knowing smile, much like the Mona Lisa smile. "This is who you are!" she said to me telepathically. Her eyes were almond shaped and beautiful and expressed an unconditional love and an ancient wisdom that was strong and knowing. Her body was in the shape of a human form, but she was glowing! She glowed with a white and golden light, with hints of blue throughout. She was luminescent! She literally glowed from within! If you've ever seen the movie Cocoon, there is a scene where the young female from another star system takes off her human skin and emerges as a glowing entity. That's what I really looked like! Absolutely stunning!

She (I) possessed a wonderful combination of strength and gentleness – a perfect balance of masculine and feminine energies. She knew all, loved all and was there to be of service to others. She possessed an inner strength and assuredness that was solid and steady, and yet a softness and quietness that radiated warmth, contentment and wisdom.

As I continued to look into her eyes, I became aware of several other entities around us. They were glowing forms also, but I couldn't see their faces. It looked as though they were wearing glowing capes that made them appear soft and willowy. I heard a voice that spoke for the whole group. It said, "You are one of us. You were the one from our soul group who chose to come here to Earth. We are proud of the work you are doing. We are here to assist you in any way. We are here to help you, but you must ask for our assistance. We love you and want to help you on this journey."

And then they all faded away.

When Laura Lyn finished the session, I explained to her what had happened. She was so excited! She said she knew something very special was happening because she could feel a strong presence in the room, way more than her usual sessions. She and I hugged each other with such happiness to have had this experience.

I'm still in awe of what I saw and heard during my Angel Ray Healing sessions. I've told many people about this visionary experience because I think it's important for all of us to know two things. One, that we are all beings of Light and Love. We all glow from within and have an inner wisdom that is there for us to tap into at any time. We are balanced entities, whole and complete. We have strength from our masculine energies – an inner strength that comes from an inner knowing of Truth. And we are soft. We have a gentleness from our feminine energies that allows us to be compassionate, warm and caring.

And secondly, we all need to recognize that we are not alone. We each have a soul group, a spiritual family, who watches over us and surrounds us with love and protection. This is our true family. We are the ones who are "away." They care deeply about our happiness and progress and are available to assist us. They want to help us in our endeavors but we must first ask for their assistance. They can not intrude and cannot assist unless asked. In the quiet time of meditation and reflection, ask your spirit family, or soul group, for guidance. Ask for assistance. Ask that they show themselves to you. Your spiritual family is here with you, waiting for your requests. They'll be so thrilled to have you acknowledge them and ask for their support.

I've tried to use this experience to help me grow spiritually. I often use my imagination to visualize glowing, luminescent bodies inside each person I see. It truly changes the way you look at people. For those we see who are angry or lost, they've truly forgotten who they are. For others, there is a glimmer of understanding inside. Sometimes your eyes will meet with someone who is seeing you as a glowing spiritual being. Your eyes communicate a knowingness of who you really are. There's such joy and magic in those special moments.

I also try to envision my own glowing form inside this physical body. I imagine my luminescent body looking out through radiant eyes at the world, at the people and at the beauties of nature. When I look through those glowing eyes, instead of my thinking, analyzing eyes, the world looks softer and gentler. I feel like I've been reborn and look through new eyes. It's like looking at the world with my heart instead of my brain. If only I could do this all the time. I forget. I forget who I really am. Even with having this wonderful, outrageous experience, I still forget who I really am. And then I breathe. And then I slow down. And then I remember who I truly am. And then I remember who you truly are, a spiritual being having a human experience. We are all glowing forms wrapped in a skin of earthly matter.

It's time for you to remember who you really are – a luminescent, spiritual being who has taken a trip to Earth to learn and grow and help others on their journey here. Wake up to the Truth of your true nature. Remember who you truly are.

For more information about Laura Lyn, please visit her website at www.angelreader.net.

HEALING THE SPIRIT

VICTIMS OF SEXUAL ABUSE OFTEN feel a great disconnect with God. Many of you may even be very angry at God for letting the abuse happen to you. I felt both of these very strongly. When the memories of my abuse surfaced in my early thirties, I was so resentful of God. I felt that He had sent this tiny baby girl to cruel and dysfunctional people to be raised in a home filled with violence, sexual abuse, lies and confusion. He abandoned me during my childhood and left me with not one unbalanced parent, but two mentally unstable individuals to be in charge of my care. "How could you?" was often my conversation with God.

Many years later, the memories of my wonderful trips into the Light as a child surfaced. Those beautiful cherubs would appear at the time of the abuse and whisk me away into the Light. God had not abandoned me, but had sent a rescue squad to relieve some of the pain of the abuse. You may not remember your angels, just like I didn't know about them for years, but you have your own set of angelic beings that have never left you. They were there for you and you survived. And they're still here. Your spirit guides and angels surround you constantly. You just don't know they're there!

Your Spirit is strong and you survived. There may be residue of the abuse left over that still clouds the brightness of your Light, but your Light still exists within you. Your Spirit may feel small, afraid, weak, ashamed or even non-existent, but I assure you it is there. You survived. Now it's time to remember who you really are and clean away the sludge left over from the abuse and let your Light shine.

This is where traditional counseling failed me. There was no healing of the Spirit. Counselors aren't permitted to speak of such matters, but must stick with proven methods and models that deal solely with the mind. They must adhere to strict guidelines and follow techniques that have solid clinical evidence of effectiveness. And yet some of my most powerful healing came from spiritual practices.

We must change the way we help people deal with sexual abuse by addressing the Mind, the Body AND the Spirit. This holistic approach allows all of the dents caused by the abuse to be healed, not just the Mind or the Body, but the Spirit also. In this way, we heal the entire person.

My hope is that you can help heal your Spirit with these techniques. My larger hope is that counselors and professors will introduce these practices into the bag of tools they give their patients for coping mechanisms and healing methods. Several of my friends are counselors and they feel so frustrated about not being able to suggest non-traditional approaches with their clients. They may sneak in a phrase or two or make a quiet suggestion, but they can't openly practice a holistic method of counseling and speak of the Spirit with the person without fear of losing their licenses. The time has come to merge the science of the mind with the power of the Spirit in helping people heal. Whether the damage is done by sexual abuse, war time battlefield experiences or some other type of traumatic incident, we can do a better job of helping the survivors reclaim their power and live a life of peacefulness.

Meditation

My first suggestion for healing the Spirit will always be meditation. As stated in previous sections, meditation helps quiet the Mind and heals the Body. It is also the main step in healing the Spirit. By sitting in the silence, we can start feeling the presence of a Divine Spirit. We can build a personal relationship with the powerful source that created us. We can start hearing the voice of the Divine Spirit we may call God, Alwah, Source Energy or whatever name you're comfortable with.

Meditation helps bring about a greater sense of self-awareness and the feeling of being more "connected" to a higher power. It helps us from feeling so alone. Meditation can help you feel a greater sense of purpose, along with the added benefit of helping you to resolve past issues that tend to get buried in the psyche. It helps you transcend what happened to you, to go beyond the day-to-day activities of your life, and see your existence from your Higher Self.

When you witness events in your life from a higher consciousness, you lift yourself up from the ego-centered existence to a deeper, more spiritual way of being. You may see a higher purpose in what happened to you or strive to bring kindness and compassion into every situation or relationship you enter. As you enter the quietness in meditation, you expand your consciousness and go beyond the basic thinking levels of your brain and reach deeper levels of wisdom and understanding. Your relationship with God is strengthened as you see things from your Higher Self. You think more with your heart than with your noisy, negative brain. You retrain your brain to be quiet, so that you can hear God's message in your heart. Whatever your faith, Christian, Buddhist, Muslim, Tao, Jewish, or no faith at all, you'll commune with God on a much deeper level when you enter the nothingness through meditation that is the unified field of God. Meditation helped lift me out of a rut of negative thinking and hopelessness to feeling optimism and peace of mind. There comes a quiet wisdom that you're not alone in your healing journey.

Meditation is not a competitive sport, but an ongoing process. As Dr. Deepak Chopra states, "Meditation is not a way of making your mind quiet. It is a way of entering into the quiet that is already there—buried under the 50,000 thoughts the average person thinks every day."

I encourage you to explore the spiritual realm in order to find and illuminate your own inner Light. Start with just 5 or 10 minutes a day. Meditate anywhere—your sofa, out in nature, your car at lunch. Consider creating a Zen room in your home or at least a Zen corner of your bedroom where you can sit and commune with your own Spirit, plus maintain a connection with the grand Spirit. Meditation is not a destination but a fascinating journey where you will become more awakened to your true self. Meditation will bring you peace. Maybe not right away, but eventually you will enter the serene inner space within you that has always existed. It's time to tap into this inner resource of spiritual blessings and grace. Your Spirit is waiting for you there.

As you start to meditate, your ego will feel threatened and rightly so. You are taking control of your life and asking the ego to sit down and be quiet. It will resist. It will resist both openly and subtly. But as long as you hold on to the identity of "victim," the ego has its hold on you. When you meditate and start to identify yourself as a wonderful spirit, the ego loses its grip on you. Stop listening to the incessant negative chatter from the ego and release the beautiful Spirit inside through meditation. Eckhart Tolle has a wonderful book called *A New Earth, Awakening to Your Life's Purpose* where he speaks so eloquently about the shift from ego to Spirit. On page 57, he states:

> Spirit is released from its imprisonment in matter. You realize your essential identity as formless, as an all-pervasive Presence, of Being prior to all forms, all identifications. You realize your true identity as consciousness itself, rather than what consciousness had identified with. That's the peace of God. The ultimate truth of who you are is not I am this or I am that, but I Am.

Go beyond the "I am a victim" consciousness to the "I Am" presence within you. Peace will then be yours.

ANGELS AND SPIRIT GUIDES

As I stood in the shower one evening, I lathered up my purple cleansing pouf with shower gel and scrubbed away the events of the day. The water felt good running down my body as it rinsed the scented bubbles from my arms and legs. I used my razor and a bar of soap and shaved under my arms - first one and then the other, and then started on my legs. I moved the shower curtain back a bit and placed my left foot on the side of the bathtub. I lathered up my left calf with the bar of Ivory soap and bent over to start shaving around my ankle.

Swish!

My right foot, which was holding most of my weight, suddenly slipped on some of the bubbles left over from the bath gel. Instantly, my head flung downward as my right foot went up behind me. With my left leg bent and angled on the side of the bathtub, I had no way of stopping my fall. My right hand was holding the razor and the fingertips on my left hand gently touched the shower curtain to my left. My face was headed for the side of the porcelain tub and there was nothing I could do about it. I was falling quickly downward with nothing to grab onto. Oh, this was going to hurt! I held my breath!

And then, in an instant, my downward fall stopped. My body suddenly became suspended in mid-air, lifted upwards, and gently came down on both feet in the middle of the tub. My body literally stopped its forward motion and reversed its direction and came safely at rest in full standing position. All of this took place in 2–3 seconds, but the entire event felt like it was in slow motion.

I stood there with my mouth open in awe of what had just happened. My heart was beating hard inside my chest both from the scare of almost falling and from the magic of the miracle that had just happened to me. I knew in that moment that I had a guardian angel.

There was no other explanation for the reversal of motion I had just experienced. My angel had defied the Laws of Gravity and had saved me from a nasty head injury. I instantly started saying "Thank You!" over and over again, mixed in with a few "Oh my God! What just happened to me?" statements. I finished shaving my legs in a blur of thoughts about angels and divine intervention and "Who's going to believe this?"

Before this experience, I had always believed in the general concept of angels but had never really felt their presence personally. However, this experience changed my life forever. I started reading about angels extensively and found the work of Dr. Doreen Virtue, an esteemed psychologist who turned her successful practice in clinical counseling into Angel Therapy. She has authored several books and has published decks of Angel Cards that I've used for years to receive messages from the angelic realm.

To help heal your Spirit, I would advise you to start working with your angels and spirit guides. This will open your heart to the angelic realm and allow the angels to help heal your damaged Spirit. Doreen's website, www.AngelTherapy.com, states the following:

"When you work with angels, you can lean upon their light to help you heal at miraculous rates and in amazing ways. The angels can help us heal physically, spiritually, emotionally, and financially."

According to Doreen we have many beings in the spiritual realm who are there to help us. I've included a brief summary of a few of her definitions of these spiritual beings from her website below:

- **Angels**—These are the beings of light created by God who respond to our calls for guidance, assistance, protection, and comfort. Ask for angels to surround you, your loved ones, your home, and your business.
- **Guardian Angel**—This is the angel who constantly stays with you, from birth until your transition back to heaven. Your guardian angel makes certain you are safe and guided always.

- **Spirit Guide**—This is a loving being who has lived upon the earth in human form. This person then received special training in the afterlife about how to become a spirit guide.

  He or she is not to interfere with your free will or make decisions for you, but is there to give you general advice, comfort, and at times warning and protection. Most spirit guides are deceased loved ones, such as grandparents, siblings, beloved friends, and parents.

- **Archangels**—These are the angels who supervise the guardian angels and other angels upon the earth. You can call upon an archangel whenever you need powerful and immediate assistance. Since angels are purely spiritual beings, they have no time or space restrictions. An archangel can help many people in different geographical locations simultaneously.

Doreen goes on to say that "Because of the 'Law of Free Will,' angels and archangels cannot intervene in our lives unless we specifically ask for their help. The only exception to this is a life-endangering situation, where we could die before our time. Otherwise, it's up to us to remember to constantly invite angels and archangels into our lives." I guess my near-fall in the bathroom was one of those life-endangering situations where the angels intervened on my behalf.

There are many ways to become aware of your angels and spirit guides. The first way is to talk to them. They're already in the room with you waiting to assist. They're waiting for you to notice them. Ask them for protection. Ask them for healing. Ask them for guidance about how to handle a particular situation. And then be open. Pay attention to a voice in your head—a gentle whisper or a thought-form that's not really yours. Try some automatic writing where you ask a question and allow yourself to start jotting down anything that comes in your head. Don't judge what you're getting, don't doubt it, just start writing. It feels silly at first, but the words will come. It may take several sittings but the angels and spirit guides want to communicate with you and it takes some practice to set our reception on a clear channel to hear them.

Ask your angels for assistance

During meditation, ask your angels and spirit guides to show themselves to you. Ask them for their names. Be open to feeling the love and tenderness that comes with their presence. By opening your awareness to the spirit realm you take giant steps in healing your Spirit. Open your heart chakra and allow the possibilities to enter your experience beyond the physical world. There's another dimension that exists where heavenly beings are waiting to help us. But first we have to ask for their assistance. Having a connection with the spirit realm allows our Spirit to expand and, ultimately, heal.

Another way to communicate with your angels and spirit guides is by asking for signs. In your morning meditation or prayer time, ask that the angels show you a sign during that day that they are listening to you. Ask them to show you a certain item, play a certain song, or have a certain person contact you during the day. Have fun with it! Be open and be aware of their presence. The more contact you have with the spirit realm, the more peace you'll feel in your Spirit.

Look for synchronicities! This is how you know you are connected to Spirit. When things start happening out of the blue, know that your angels and spirit guides are working with you.

NATURE

During the time that I was experiencing my flashbacks and going to weekly counseling sessions, I was suffering from extreme stress. My heart was heavy and sad. My body was tired and lifeless. My spirit was weak and fragile. During these times I found that if I worked in my flower beds, I felt tremendously better. There is something so therapeutic about having your hands in the dirt. To feel the earth with your feet and your fingers brings such a calming effect and makes your Spirit feel at ease.

Being in nature is an easy way to feel close to God. Take a walk amongst the snowflakes. Remove your shoes and stand on the grass. Sit down on Mother Earth and lean against a tree. Slowly step your way along the stones in a stream. Plant a flower with gentle mindfulness that God has created all of life with such wonderful design and purpose. Row a kayak around the edge of a lake. Sit on a park bench in the rain. Slow down and soak in the healing qualities of the earth. She is there as a nurturing Mother to revive your Spirit and ease your burdens.

Dr. Warren Grossman wrote a book called *To Be Healed by the Earth*. An accomplished psychologist, he contracted a deadly parasite while vacationing in Brazil and went home to die. While waiting for the end to come, he went outside and lay on the Earth. And Mother Earth healed him. He now operates the Warren Grossman School of Healing, a non-profit teaching center in Ohio through which he trains people in an active, step-by-step process to access the Earth's energy and deliberately open their hearts. The Earth healed his body, and I believe it can heal our mind and spirit, as well.

Spiritual Community

I had been looking for a church to feed my Spirit, but was not at all successful in finding something that felt right. I started taking classes at a local yoga center and would go to lunch with some of the teachers and classmates afterwards. Our spiritual discussions were so amazing! I loved all the new information I was learning and I loved the gentleness and wisdom displayed by these people. My community of spiritual friends continued to grow as I explored various religions and spiritual paths. Our discussions and book studies allowed my Spirit to grow in leaps and bounds as I found my place in the spirit realm. I found a 'knowing' in me that this was Truth in its highest form.

If you don't have a place of worship that is nurturing to your soul, start looking for a new spiritual community. Check out your local yoga centers, find a holistic or spiritual center in your city, check Google for meditation classes in your area—do something to find people of 'like mind' who want to grow spiritually. A friend of mine moved to a small town in Canada and felt very alone with no spiritual friends around to discuss life's happenings. She placed a small ad in the local newspaper about looking for people to discuss spiritual issues on a weekly basis. Thirteen people showed up! They all had been looking for a safe place to explore their spirituality and were so excited about the new friends they had found. Some were even acquaintances, but didn't know the other was interested in spiritual topics. It didn't feel safe to bring up such topics so they all felt so alone. They've now found a spiritual community to share ideas and delight in God's wonder.

Find a spiritual community of some sort to help you on this journey. Find your Spirit in the company of others. It's so much more fun that way!

I've used many avenues to revive my Spirit. Through meditation, contact with my angels and spirit guides, being in nature and having spiritual friends, I've learned to feel that connection with the Spirit world, with God. I feel my own Spirit. I know that I am a spiritual being having a human experience. I feel important and yet humbled by the mystery of it all. I feel part of the majestic Oneness of the Universe and yet know that I am just a small part in the grand scheme of things. And I am now okay with that. I know my place—I know that I am part of something marvelous, even if I don't know the whole story. And I still continue to learn. And my Spirit continues to blossom into the beautiful essence it was meant to be. Actually, my Spirit has always been beautiful and blossoming. I've just awakened to the beauty of my own essence. And so can you.

Eckhart Tolle states on page 214 of *A New Earth* that:

> The joy of Being, which is the only true happiness, cannot come to you through any form, possession, achievement, person, or event—through anything that happens. That joy cannot *come* to you—ever. It emanates from the formless dimension within you from consciousness itself and thus is one with who you are.

Awaken to your Spirit by quieting the ego mind and inviting the still, small voice to tea. Enter the silence and experience a peace that passes all understanding.

Part IV:
The Unity Principles

Principles of the Unity Church

In the 1890's, Charles and Myrtle Fillmore started a prayer group that eventually developed into the Unity Church. Today there are millions of followers of this new thought movement around the world. They believe that God is a loving source of all that is and that there are many paths to this Divine Source. The Unity Church honors all religions and follows Jesus as a Way-Shower to the truth of who we are. They believe that the more we awaken to our divine nature, the more fully God expresses in and through our lives.

There was a small Unity church in my area that I had heard about from a couple of people. They said that I may enjoy the teachings of the Unity philosophy. I checked the phone book and found the address. It was in Massillon, a town about 10 miles west of where I was living. I drove out there one day to locate it and found it hidden behind a group of trees. It was hard to see from the busy street. What I found was a ranch house sitting atop a mound on several acres of property. The parking lot was behind the house and you walked up a long flight of stairs dug into the hillside made of railroad ties and paving bricks. I sat in the parking lot and looked at it. It felt weird, like I would be entering someone's home. And there was an eeriness that surrounded the place. I wasn't as aware of my intuition as I am now, but I did listen to it that day. I didn't go back to the church for several years.

Then Divine Order played its part. In July of 2004, I moved into my current house at Willowdale Lake, which is located about 5 miles north of the Unity church. My immediate neighbor was an elderly gentleman named Don Myers. His wife Elaine had passed on between the time I bought the house and actually moved in, so I never got to meet her. Don had been the music director at the Unity church for years and had traveled around the world singing about the beautiful Unity message. He had a wonderful baritone voice and I got to hear him singing only once. He was inside his home with the windows open and singing the most beautiful song. I was working in my yard and his wonderful voice came traveling along the breeze out into the open grass and out onto the lake. It was awe inspiring and I sat back from my weeding and listened to the beautiful sound of his voice. Later, I talked to Don and heard his story about being associated with Unity Church and his travels abroad singing at Unity churches worldwide. A few weeks later, he brought me a copy of a Unity publication called the *Daily Word*. For those not acquainted with the *Daily Word*, it is a bi-monthly publication printed by the Unity Church. Along with its wonderful true stories, it has daily affirmations, short paragraphs with thoughts for the day and scripture passages. The affirmations in the *Daily Word* are also available free online. I've included the website at the end of this chapter. I loved the messages that I read each day and decided to attend a service at the church.

So, one Sunday morning I showered and got dressed and drove to the Unity church. I made sure to show up right at the scheduled time of the service so that I could slip into the back row of seats without being noticed. I sat down in one of the chairs in the back and said 'Hi' to the woman beside me. She mentioned her name and welcomed me to the church. The music had already started so there wasn't much time for talking. As I read the bulletin, I noticed the list of people on the Board of Directors. There was someone on the list with her first name, so I pointed to the name in the bulletin,

Rosetta Van Campen, and showed it to her. I then pointed at her and gave her a questioning look that said "Is that you?" She smiled and nodded "Yes." The minister, Rev. Steve Colladay, welcomed us to the church and settled us in for a period of meditation. Meditation! They meditate right here in church!!? Oh, this is so cool!

So I closed my eyes and listened to his strong voice guide us into the quiet. The peacefulness could actually be felt. I listened carefully to his sermon and loved the message of love and inclusiveness. He told of how the world is like a wheel with God at the center and that each spoke of the wheel represents a path to God. He said there are many paths to God, no one more right or holy than another. He went on to say that one spoke of the wheel was Hindu, another Muslim; one was for Buddhism and another Native American. One spoke of the wheel was Christian and that was the way, or the teachings, that the Unity church followed, but that they respected all paths to God.

Wow! This was music to my ears. There was acceptance of many types of beliefs and he wasn't saying that theirs was the only way. After the wonderful service was completed, I was approached by several of the people in attendance. They welcomed me and asked me to come back. I felt like I was home. I've heard so many people say that about Unity and now about the Merging Hearts Holistic Center. Something resonates within you when you know you're in the right place. It feels like home when the Truth is spoken.

That first Sunday, I looked around the church for my neighbor, Don Myers, and didn't see him anywhere. It was a small church with only forty or so people there, but I couldn't place him, since there were so many people there in his age range. Plus, the church was a former house and broken up into small rooms and different doorways and hallways, so after the service it was often hard to see everyone at one time. I asked someone if Don was there that day and they looked around, but couldn't see him either. I was to find out later that Don had become seriously ill and never was able to return to the church. Although we lived beside each other, we never got to attend a church service together. His health continued to fail and he passed on to the other side a few short months later. I was sad that we had never had the chance to sit with one another during a service, but he served his purpose in getting me to go to the Unity church. I did mention to him one day in the yard before he died that I had started going to church and he seemed very pleased. He nodded quietly and smiled. I attended his Memorial Service held at the church. During the many messages and beautiful songs, there was one pole lamp on the stage that kept flickering. We all smiled knowing that Don was telling us he was here with us. The light never flickered before or after that service!

I became a regular attendee of the Unity Church of Truth in Massillon, OH. I met many wonderful friends there and eventually served on the Board of Trustees. I fell in love with the teachings of the Unity Church. They felt so right from the first time I heard them and they continue to hold true for me to this day.

The Five Basic Principles of Unity can be so helpful to people who have been sexually abused and neglected. They help restore our sense of self worth and give us hope for the future. The Unity principles are also very healing for those of us who were raised under the damaging, fundamental Christian beliefs of being separate from God and filled with original sin. This chapter is devoted to these wonderful Unity principles. I'll describe each tenet and then describe how each principle played a part in my healing process from the sexual abuse. My wish is that you find them helpful as well.

THE FIVE BASIC PRINCIPLES OF UNITY ARE:

1. God is absolute good and everywhere present.
2. We have a spark of divinity within. Our very essence is of God and we are therefore inherently good.
3. We create our experiences by the activity of our minds. Everything has its start in thought.
4. Prayer is creative thinking that heightens the connection

with God-Mind and therefore brings forth wisdom, healing, prosperity, and everything good.

5. Knowing and understanding the Laws of Life, also called TRUTH, are not enough. We must live the truth we know.

So now, let's take each of these principles and dig deeper into their meaning and their application to the healing process for victims of sexual abuse.

First Unity Principle

God is absolute good and everywhere present.

Unity believes in a truly loving God. A God who guides and directs, forgives, then guides and directs and forgives, again, and again, and again. This statement made perfect sense to me and reflected what I had felt for years. I'll look at the two parts for this statement separately. First, the declaration that 'God is absolute good' felt so very right. I had always questioned the conflicting belief systems in so many churches that God loved me and yet that same God would send me to burn in hell for eternity if I didn't do things according to the church. Burn for Eternity?! Sheesh! I can see that there may be consequences for my actions, but burning for eternity in hell seemed a bit harsh. How could you deem God as a "loving" entity when he would punish you for eternity for making a mistake? This conflict in ideology always caused me to question the validity of the church.

God loves us in all ways and will never send us to hell. In fact, it is my belief and the belief of the Unity church that there is no hell. There's no terrible burning pit where folks are forever disciplined for mistakes they have made in the way they lived their life. Many academic and historical documents now show us that hell is a made-up place, created by early church leaders to control their followers with fear. Hell is a myth they borrowed from other ancient tales. They twisted Jesus' true teachings and incorporated this place of eternal damnation in his stories. God never made a place called hell. God loves us and gives us many, many chances to learn our lessons. God is love. Period. God is absolute love. And love is all there is. Love is what makes the world go round. Love conquers all. Love is perfect and forgives perfectly. God is not some Wizard of Oz character who is ready to judge us for what we may or may not have done. God does not judge us by a doctrine created by men many years ago. God is absolute good. He/She is loving, always and forever, to everyone regardless of the mistakes we have made or the religious path we choose to follow.

The first part of this statement, *God is absolute good*, helped me in so many ways. One of the troubling questions I brought up to my Sunday School teachers at the Baptist church was, "Why would the people of foreign countries, who may not have ever heard of Jesus, be punished for not worshiping him?" I further always questioned any religious path that stated that its way was the *only way* to heaven. To finally hear that *God is absolute good* just felt right. I had always squirmed a little when I heard about the vengeful God and his hypocritical ways of damnation. But upon hearing the statement that *God is absolute good*, came a knowing deep inside my chest that what I was hearing was the Truth.

The second part of this principle states that *God is everywhere present*. This statement is so important, because in many religions, and especially in most forms of Christianity, we are taught that God is somewhere out there or up there in heaven. God is often portrayed as a man, a distant entity that we must pray to, and be afraid of, and request things from, but mostly we needed to be afraid of him, afraid of his judgments.

God is everywhere present! God is a part of every human, every other living thing and is part of the ethers all around us. God made the Earth, the solar system, our Universe, and all the other star systems within space. God exists within the tiniest molecule of rich fertile soil and the beautiful tree bark of the sycamore. God exists within the stamen of the tiger lily and the seed of a Big Boy tomato. God is found within the tiny baby girl with curly auburn locks and the elderly homeless man with graying, dirty hair. God is present in the mountain stream and the trout that playfully swim there. There is no place that God is not. God is in the air that sags heavy with smog and the air that is electrically charged from a lightning bolt. We are surrounded by God and his love. We are filled with God and his love. We are not alone to fight our way through this existence. God is here among us, within us, around us at all times. When we wake up and see the Truth about who and where God is, our life changes dramatically. We are not isolated globs of clay who must beseech God for forgiveness. We're not isolated beings struggling on our own. We're wonderful creations of God surrounded by other wonderful creations of God. We are surrounded by Love at all times, in all ways. There is a giant web of consciousness that is God. It is something that we swim in and It is there for our discovery and use. *God is absolute good and everywhere present!*

There is a wonderful spiritual book called *A Fish Made of Water* by Michael Olin Hitt. That title so brilliantly describes how we are made of the very same essence of God as the environment we live in. We swim within the very essence of God. Everything is made of the same loving energy that radiates from God. I once heard an analogy that it's like everything is made of chocolate. Some of the chocolate has solidified into trees, some into humans, some into cars, but eventually it all melts down to liquid again.

For victims of abuse, it is refreshing to hear that God is good and that He/She is there for us. It means that there is someone solid and strong and loving that will help us manage the everyday struggles of life on Earth. There is someone to lean on when the journey gets rough…someone loving and kind and wise. God is here within us, listening to our concerns, hearing our pleas for strength and guidance and more importantly, is answering us back. As we begin to acknowledge this God of Love that lives within us and surrounds us always, we can hear the gentle guidance that comes with a direct connection to God, to a good and gentle Spirit. We don't have to be in church to talk to God. We don't have to be on our knees to hear God's voice. God is everywhere—in the grocery store, in the woods, in your car, on your patio. We have 24-hour access to a good and holy presence that will calm us, give us direction and free us from the shame and guilt that comes with sexual abuse. Ask God to lift the depression that clouds your existence. Ask God to help you deal with the anger you feel towards your abuser and towards all those who covered it up. Ask the Holy Spirit to take away your feelings of unworthiness, your feelings of being dirty or your feelings of being used and damaged. Ask for guidance in your relationships. Ask for help with your co-dependency issues. Ask for assistance with behaviors that exhibit the lack of value you have for yourself. God can help you at any time and at any place.

This principle, *God is absolute good and everywhere present*, is a real shift in thinking. I used to feel alone in the world, surviving the best I could all by myself. But I'm not alone to heal the emotional and psychological and physical wounds created from the abuse. God is love and that Love is there to help me heal, to help you heal. You are surrounded by Love. Reach out and touch it. Know that there are loving entities in the form of angels and spirit guides, sent by God, to help you on your journey. Know in your heart that God loved you before you left the Spirit realm, He/She loves you now, and He/She will love you when you return to the Spirit realm. God loves you, always. We may have suffered at the hands of an abuser, but God does not want us to suffer the rest of our lives with the guilt, shame, anxiety and depression that often comes with abuse. With God's help, I lifted above these emotional scars and so can you. You can live a life that is happy, light, and joyful! And knowing that *God is absolute good and everywhere present* helped me achieve that happy life.

To make this first Unity principle more personal, say **"God is absolute good. God is present with me everywhere I go."**

Second Unity Principle

We have a spark of divinity within. Our very essence is of God and we are therefore inherently good.

This statement was pretty amazing to me. Here was a church telling me that I was good! Better than that, they said I was Divine! This second Unity principle proclaims that God, that Spark of Divinity, is within us. I have a Spark of Divinity within me. You have a Spark of Divinity within you. Every single human being has a Spark of Divinity within them. Even if you can't see it in yourself, it's there. Even if you can't see it in another, it's there. God is not out there or up there, but within! He/She resides within your very soul. Your Divinity is the very essence of your being. It is the very essence of God. And since God is good, so are you!

Most churches are very good at making us feel shame and guilt for being worthless sinners. Many of the Christian faiths tell us we are filled with original sin. They purport that each human being inherently lacks a presence of God and that everything we do in our life is to beseech God for forgiveness for being a sinner. We're told we must be saved! Even the beautiful song "Amazing Grace" states that God's grace could "save a wretch like me." I was told that Jesus died on the cross for me to wash away my sins! I often wondered, *What did I do that was so bad that someone had to die for me?* I'm kind, honest, and trustworthy. Again, I questioned the Sunday School teachers, "What did I do that was so terrible to be filled with original sin? What did I do that God sent his only begotten son to die for me?" And the answer I got was "You were made that way. All humans are weak. All are sinners who have come short of the glory of God."

"Well," I would respond, "God made me, so why did he make me a sinner?"

All I got were blank stares and open mouths. They would quickly change the subject or quote another Bible verse at me. I could never understand how someone could look at a tiny infant and think they were filled with original sin. How could we take a precious three-year-old and see them as anything but a perfect, delightful child of God?

When I asked my Sunday School teachers about this, I often got the answer that "Well, no, children are different. It's not until the age of accountability that they are held responsible for their behavior, and ultimately, their salvation." Well, now I've never had children, so I can't claim to know everything about adolescents. But I have been an educator for many years having taught hundreds and hundreds of teenagers in middle schools, junior highs, and high schools, including after-school programs for at-risk teenagers living in gang-infested, drug-dealing environments. There is not a one of them that I ever saw as filled with original sin. **Never.** I may have seen scared and angry teens who lashed out in defense of being forgotten and unloved in their everyday world, but I've never seen a teenager filled with sin. There are lonely and anxious teens who behave in unflattering ways in order to fit in and be accepted or loved by a group. There are teens who escape their hollow existence and the burdens of caring for younger siblings and alcoholic or drug-addicted parents, and turn to alcohol or drugs themselves. But I have never seen any young person filled with original sin.

Whenever you see any person behaving in a way that is cruel or greedy, angry or uncaring, rude or mean, look beyond the behavior and view that person as someone who is scared. Ask yourself, what happened to that person that made them so scared and angry? What happened to them that turned that Spark of Divinity into a flicker that no one can see any more? We are all creations of God and we all have a Spark of Divinity within us. We are the very essence of God. We are inherently good! Good to the core! Next time you see a teenager, a child, an adult, tell them they have a Spark of the Divine Spirit within them. You may just change their life!

This thought, that I have a Spark of Divinity within me, helped me to rid myself of the shame that the sexual abuse laid upon me. Victims of sexual abuse wear this heavy cloak of shame around all the time. It's like wearing a heavy woolen cape that is soaked with water. Its weight is profound and tiresome, and very smelly. I was constantly trying to hide it from people, even myself. When I heard that I had a Spark of the Divine in me, it was as if I knew it to be true! And as I practiced telling myself just that, "I have a Spark of the Divine within me," it felt like that heavy, water-laden wool cape slid off my shoulders. I felt a lightness of being. I felt okay about myself. I felt I was likable. I felt I was lovable. Able to love and accept love. And then I would forget about that Spark (the ego is good at making you forget about your Spark!) and I would put that ugly, water-logged cape back on and walk around for awhile. And then I would hear that phrase again—*I have a Spark of Divinity within me*. I have a piece of God within me! And the cape of shame would slide off again.

This process of ridding myself of my shame took many years. It took many reminders of how special I am in the eyes of God for me to keep the cape off for long periods of time. It took a lot of repetitions for ME to believe how special and Divine I am. We humans forget that, even if we have so-called normal childhoods. Our society is always telling us that we're not good enough. All marketing is based on igniting the fear within you that you're not good enough, so you need this shampoo, this tennis shoe, this car, this house, this vacation, this job, this beer to fit in and be okay. And those who have been abused have extra layers of unworthiness to shed. Every affirmation you say peels another layer of unworthiness away. It's like peeling that onion, one layer at a time, until you find your Spark of Divinity within.

It took many daily prompts through affirmations, spiritual books, uplifting songs and professional counseling to find that Divinity within. And there are still times when I feel an absence of Spirit. I'll feel apprehensive in a situation or unsure about meeting someone. I'll feel less than I really am. And I go back to the saying, "I have a Spark of Divinity within me. I am a child of God" and the peace and sureness is mine again. Knowing that I am a piece of the Divine essence isn't arrogance or being uppity, that's not what I mean by knowing that I'm special or precious. It's knowing that I am as special as anyone else, and everyone else. It's a *knowing* that I am equal in the eyes of God. When you, a victim of sexual abuse, are able to shed your cloak of shame, you will see a wonderful emergence of beauty and confidence from within. When you can identify, even for a moment, that you have a Spark of Divinity within you, you will start to shine like the wonderful Light of God that you are! Your Spark may have been diminished and subdued, but it is still there. No matter how much you think your Spark has been snuffed out, your Spark is still there, waiting to be acknowledged. Waiting to burn brighter. Ask God to help you find it. Meditate and ask God to let you feel your Divine Spark within your Sacred Heart. I often feel my Divine Spark by being in nature and feeling the God Spirit all around me.

Volunteer and help others and you'll feel that Spark brighten. Tell yourself every day that you have a Spark of Divinity within you. And there will come a day when you actually believe it. You will **know** it. You will **own** it. And the cloak of shame will come off and stay off. Continue your affirmations. Be with people who are positive and uplifting and treat you with respect and kindness. Treat yourself with respect and kindness. Read the books that I've included in the suggested reading list. Listen to the healing music listed in Appendix A that have positive lyrics and soothing melodies. All of these will help you rid yourself of the cloak of shame forever. Attend a Unity church in your area or another metaphysical place of worship that teaches these same holistic, life-affirming principles. Start a support group or book study group that affirms the Spark within.

I have a Spark of Divinity within me! Type this out, write it down, and paste it everywhere! This one thing will help you recover from your abuse faster than anything else. It will help you reclaim your life. It will reverse the feelings of unworthiness! Know it! Feel it! Even if you don't believe it or if the thought even repulses you at first, say it anyway, every day. You may not even be able to say it out loud at first. Then just look at it every day. Then say just the first word, then the first two. Move slowly if you have to. Work towards saying "I have a Spark of Divinity within me!" out loud every single day, many times a day. Try saying it out loud while looking yourself in the eyes in a mirror. Your ego is in control and loves that cloak of shame. But you can rid yourself of the shame and feelings of low self-esteem forever by claiming your Divine power and claiming your heritage—as a sparkling child of God! Type or write out this phrase on paper, and say it out loud. I have a Spark of Divinity within me! Tape this affirmation on your bathroom mirror, your computer screen, your dashboard, ...wherever!

So, let's make this second Unity principle more personal by changing a few words: **I have a Spark of Divinity within me. My very essence is of God and therefore, I am inherently good and worthwhile!**

Third Unity Principle

We create our experiences by the activity of our minds. Everything has its start in thought.

The main premise of this philosophy is that we create our physical life in our mind first. We imagine what will happen and then it is created all around us. Most of us do not know about this Law of the Universe, but it is working at all times. It works whether we know about it or not. We just were never told about it. If we imagine or worry about our daily existence getting more chaotic or lacking in some way, we send this message out to the Universe, and it responds to us, giving us chaos and shortages. If we imagine our world as being peaceful and abundant, the Universe hears us, and brings us peaceful and bountiful surroundings. This Law of Attraction applies to how we see ourselves and others on a daily basis, and also to the larger world we live in. It is working whether we are aware of it or not. Whatever we focus our attention on, will manifest in our lives, good or bad. The Universe doesn't judge what we think about. It just gives us what we think about. We create our world with our thoughts.

This principle escaped me for many years. The idea that we create our reality was not something I could grasp. It went over my head to the point that I didn't even think about it. While I was attending Unity Church of Truth, I didn't hear much about this line of philosophy. It wasn't until I was working as the Director of the Fieldcrest Holistic Learning Center in 2007 when the movie "The Secret" came out that I started giving it more thought. I showed the movie at the Center and even scheduled a workshop based on the teachings. It also brought out the teachings of Esther and Jerry Hicks with the Law of Attraction. I had read a little about their work and had watched some of their videos.

Of course, this Law applies to everyone but I'll apply it here to victims of sexual abuse. As victims, we often have a very low sense of self. We don't value ourselves and we don't expect others to value us either. So it's this expectation that plays itself out in our world. Since I expected men to be unreliable and untrustworthy, I attracted men who were unreliable and untrustworthy. I expected men to break my heart, so I attracted men into my world who would eventually break my heart. But when I changed my mind about men, when I changed my thinking about the characteristics of men, I attracted a different kind of man into my life. When I stopped 'male-bashing' and respected all men, I began to attract better and better men. As I began to really use this Law to my advantage, I wanted to attract a man who *knew* about the Law of Attraction and all the other metaphysical teachings. And so I did. I met an attractive man, who was intelligent, respectable, very knowledgeable about meditation, and the teachings of the New Thought movement. He *knew* all about these ideas, but he didn't truly *live* the philosophies of the spiritual world. His ego was still very much in control of his life. It became evident in the way he treated servers in restaurants, the way he treated me eventually and the way that he needed to be in the limelight all the time. He once told me his goal was to write a book and be famous and strut around in linen clothes like Deepak

Chopra! Well, eventually I told him that I really didn't think that Deepak ever strutted his stuff. Deepak appeared to me to be a very humble man. That relationship didn't survive, but that was really okay. I had learned what it was like to be with a man who was on his spiritual journey and was still learning. Hey, we're all still learning. We never stop learning. So, I put it out to the Universe that I wanted a man who both talked and lived a spiritual existence. One of the ways of creating your intentions is to make a list of the things you want. Write them down or type it out. Then put the list away. Don't keep asking for them. Don't wonder "how" they'll ever come into your world. Just expect them to show up! So, I made a list of the characteristics of the man I wanted to share my life with.

Here's what I put on my list:

- Handsome
- Employed
- Kind
- Honest
- Single
- Lives a metaphysical life
- Sexy

Within a few months, I met Wayne through an online dating service. He's handsome, employed, kind, honest, single, lives a metaphysical life and he's sexy. He's everything on my list! We've been happy together ever since. I intended to meet a man with those qualities, and I did.

I have to add here that when I was making my list, I wanted to add that the man be wealthy. But then I thought to myself that I was being greedy and materialistic, so I took that characteristic off my list. My thoughts about money were that I didn't deserve to have wealth in my life and that wanting money was not spiritual. Hah! Was I wrong! Everything is spiritual! It's the meaning we attach to things, such as money, that makes it not spiritual. I come from a long line of folks who think that life is hard and money is just out of our reach. One of my family's sayings were "I'd rather be happy, than rich." That type of thinking just keeps you poor. And what's wrong with being happy and rich? And who said rich people aren't happy? Not that money brings happiness, but I know a lot of financially-struggling people who are not happy. So part of my learning has been to see money as a medium of exchange. It's simply energy. There is no limit to the supply of money in the world for me or for anyone else. It's our thinking about money that either brings it into our life or keeps it away. By not including it on the list, I kept wealth from being part of our lives. And so Wayne is not wealthy.

The second part of this principle states, *"Everything has its start in thought."* When you really want to take charge of your life you need to control what thoughts you are thinking. It's not a 24-hour job of monitoring every thought. That'll drive you crazy. But you definitely need to think about what you want in your life, versus what you *don't* want in your life. There are many techniques that can be utilized to bring what you want into manifestation. You can make vision boards, create detailed lists, or envision yourself actually using an item or living within a certain set of circumstances. These techniques work for manifesting material goods, relationships, home life, working conditions, business activities…anything! What I put out there to the Universe, is what it gives back to me. *Everything has its start in thought.*

There are many things that can stop the process or flow: Doubt, Fear, Sarcasm, Negativity. All of these can tell the Universe that you aren't sure if you want that new partner, a new job, a new home, or whatever. One of the most helpful analogies I've heard is this: If I order an item online, for example, a book from Amazon.com, I *expect* the item to show up on my pink and periwinkle front porch within a few days. I don't worry about it. I don't keep checking the delivery schedule to see where it is now. I don't get back online each day and order another one, or two or three. I know it's coming and have faith that it will arrive in good condition and on time. And it does! If I envision it getting lost or damaged, it does! The Universe doesn't care what I'm thinking about, it will simply manifest my thoughts into things or situations.

There will be several of you who are thinking that spiritual people shouldn't be materialistic. We shouldn't want so many things. And I used to think that too. There are plenty of religions who feel poverty is a shorter path to godliness. Well, it just isn't so. The Universe will provide to everyone. There's no need to be so frugal that it hurts. If a new warm sweater will bring me comfort in the cold Ohio winters, there's nothing wrong with wanting warm suitable clothing.

On the other hand, if I am wanting to impress others with how many sweaters I have or what name brand they are, then I'm not being so spiritual. This applies to homes, cars, relationships and toys, whatever your toy of choice happens to be. If it will make me happy, bring ease and joy into my life, why not bring it into fruition? God wants us to be happy! Not struggling. Not poor. Not weary. Not depressed. Not sad. Happy! A new convertible can make you happy, but only to an extent. You must have that Spark of the Divine burning brightly inside to be truly happy. The ragtop just makes it a whole lot more fun!

But now let's take this manifesting idea to another level. As a victim of childhood sexual abuse, I carried with me a certain amount of victim consciousness. I didn't know what that was, so there was no way I was able to be aware of it or change it. Victim thinking is the viewpoint or perspective in which I viewed myself and the world where I would project victim-like thoughts into my future. I did this most of my life and I didn't know I was doing it. My parents were great at it and so was I. "Playing the victim" means you constantly look at how life gives you the short end of the stick. You're almost anticipating bad things to happen to you. You don't expect much out of life. Below is a short list of victim-style thinking. If you can recognize any of these victim thoughts as being yours, then it's time to change your thinking. Victim thinking includes:

- Nothing ever goes my way.

- He'll leave me just like all the rest.
- I'll never get the promotion (or raise, or recognition, or a new job)
- Whatever!
- It's their fault!
- All the good guys are married or gay!
- I'll never be able to take a vacation!
- If I didn't have bad luck, I'd have no luck at all.
- Life is just one struggle after another.
- My car always breaks down just when I get a little money in the bank.
- It's always chaotic around my family.
- My boss hates me.
- It wouldn't do any good anyway.
- My coworkers are out to get me.
- What's the use! Nothing good ever happens to me.
- I never win anything!
- I'll never get ahead!
- I knew it was too good to be true!
- I always get sick in the Spring!

When I was reciting the above list of lies, because that's what they really are, my life reflected those thoughts.

Besides not expecting much out of life, victim thinking also led me to feel offended so easily. It's like I was expecting someone to discount me and I was ready to be angry about it. I was already pissed off before the event even happened. My defenses were up, ready for battle, so that I would not be abused again. So when a man didn't call when he said he would, I was ready with my "Men are such jerks!" statement and would instantly be offended and angry. Then I'd feel the sadness creep in and would begin more of the internal negative talk. If he did call later on, I would be very indignant and critical, not giving him a chance to explain himself or apologize. What a nasty cycle of thinking to be in. I played the victim role very well.

We need healthy boundaries for sure, but jumping down someone's throat for imagined indiscretions doesn't lead to intimacy. The ego is very good at keeping this victim thinking alive. The ego is still in charge if we are constantly mired in anger, sadness, guilt, defensiveness, and hopelessness. If we eliminate the victim thinking style of thoughts from our internal dialogue and replace them with more life-affirming thoughts, our Divine Spark burns a little brighter, our true Self emerges and the ego starts to wither away. We have to change our thoughts in order to change our lives.

In my current job, I often have to fly to client sites around the country. It's interesting to hear my coworkers talk about their experiences with missed flights, lost luggage or rude passengers. They state, "I always have trouble when I travel." They think they're talking about the past but they're actually creating the future. They're setting their intention and creating a pattern of events for future flights that there will be "trouble when I travel." And they do. The same people consistently have canceled flights, bad weather, or some other type of mishap when away on business or personal travel. I now say, "My travel is easy. My flights are safe and on time. I arrive at my destination with ease." For the most part, I have good flights with no travel problems at all. My thoughts create my reality.

Now I'd like to introduce you to Grand Mother Universe, the manifesting part of Spirit. She's standing there with her hands on her hips and listening to my thoughts and conversations, waiting to fulfill my every dream. She's standing there wondering, "Now I have all this good stuff in my pantry that's earmarked just for Jeanne. And there she goes with that victim thinking and requesting all this poverty and loneliness and struggle and emotional pain and chaos. I'm obligated by the Universal Laws of God to give her exactly what she thinks about, so here goes: One crummy coworker, a rusted muffler pipe, a critical relative, and another loser for a boyfriend. That's what she asked for, so I have to give it to her. She's expecting it!" So, UPS (Universal Postal System) of the quantum world brings my packages and dumps them on my doorstep: A coworker who yells at me, a very loud Pontiac, an aunt who minimizes my story, and another sleazy guy who cheats on me. And then I whine! I moan about my sorrows and cry in my beer and find friends who will commiserate how tough life is! This is what I expected. This is what I intended. This is what I manifested with my thoughts.

But this can all change, because now we know about Grand Mother Universe and the quantum physics of the Universal Postal System! Start putting in your orders for inner peace and harmony. Sit down and write your list of intentions. Place your order for abundance—prosperity of all sorts—with cash, ideas, love, travel, friends, activities, food, clothing, cars—whatever! Grand Mother Universe has a big pantry full of things waiting just for you! Everyone has their own pantry full of great stuff, just waiting for them. You're not taking anything away from anyone else. Surround yourself with friends who are upbeat and positive and give you healthy advice when you need it. Speaking of friends, I found that I had to find a whole new group of friends while progressing through my healing journey. It was really hard giving up the old set of friends, one by one, and finding new, more positive, friends. But it was necessary to be with people who were not negative and were not encased in victim thinking.

Imagine yourself as being slim, healthy and strong and expect it to be. See yourself with a cute partner who is loving, kind and spiritual and will support you on your healing journey. Buy that sexy nightgown in anticipation of the wonderful man who is going to enter your life! And then expect him to arrive! Get excited about the life you are going to be leading soon. Because it's coming! Grand Mother Universe is no longer standing there with her hands on her hips wondering why in the world you are ordering another fight with your neighbor. She's grinning from ear to ear as she's boxing up lots of love and happiness for you and has called UPS to come pick them up. She's sending envelopes containing airline tickets, concert tickets, workshop tickets and lots of cash. She has cars, boats, furniture and homes just waiting for your signal to ship them your way. She has ordered your perfect mate and has him on his way. And her most prized shipment is a big box of 'Inner Peace.'

What you see in your mind's eye is what you will create in your world. So choose to think about the kind of world you want. Envision the surroundings, the people, and the activities that you want in your life. Then close your eyes and feel the feelings of being in that space with those people, doing those things. That's how you communicate with Grand Mother Universe. She picks up those vibes and ships your orders to you.

Victims of sexual abuse tend to suffer from loads of negative self-talk and often project into the future further negative situations. I so often would create these terrible scenarios in my mind about how a future situation would go. For example, I might need to talk to my boss about the amount of work that I'm trying to juggle. Before I knew about Grand Mother Universe, I would have imagined myself going into the boss's office, telling him my plight and expecting him to say "Too bad. That's just the way it is. You'll have to live with it. And by the way, I'd like you to handle the Barnes case also." I could see myself walking out of his office, ready to cry and feeling totally dejected and belittled. I'd feel put-upon and hopeless, overworked and undervalued, and thinking, *See, what's the use in trying.* I'd have this whole movie picture acted out in my mind before I ever went in. And of course, that's how it usually transpired. That's what I ordered, so that's what I got. But now, I have a whole new way of envisioning what's going to happen. Now I close my eyes, see myself entering my boss's office and hear myself explaining in a confident manner how my workload has become too overwhelming. I can see my boss listening carefully to me and seeing my point of view. I see myself eventually walking out of his office with a smile on my face and a solution in hand. I try not to get attached to a particular solution, because Grand Mother Universe may have an even better solution than I can even think of. If I envision that I just want the two new customers transferred to someone else, I won't get the great new assistant that Grand Mother Universe has in the wings for me and a new raise to boot for all my hard work!

Great athletes use this Law of Attraction all the time. They envision the perfect swing on the golf course, the perfect pass on the football field, the perfect pole vault on the track and field course, the perfect return on the tennis court... it goes on forever! Now you can do it too!

My friend John Davis, the famous *John of Peniel*, has a wonderful way of manifesting just what he wants. He always says: "Thank you God, for the _____ I am about to receive." He always starts with gratitude and then ends with expectation. And it works! View more about John at www.johnofpeniel.com.

People who have been abused allow their victim complex to spill out onto every aspect of their life. We have this strong ego mind that belittles us and makes us feel that everything bad in life will happen to us. We don't expect much, so we don't get much. Start expecting good things to show up in your life. Expect to be thinner! Expect to have the assets you need! Expect to be in a loving relationship! Expect that you will be healed of your trauma! Expect that you will be peaceful and calm! Don't just wish it, expect it! Get excited about it! A major part of what *The Secret* and the Hicks material have to say about manifesting what you want is to get the emotional side of you involved.

I'm deeply involved with a spiritual organization called The Merging Hearts Holistic Center in Canton, OH. I've had a vision of a circular building that we'll one day inhabit. I'm so excited about the new building that we'll eventually be in. I have no idea how we're going to buy it, build it or obtain it. I only know it will happen and that someday I'm going to open the magnificent stained-glass doors into that wonderful circular building and be surrounded by glorious lilting music, beautiful blooming flowers, stunning waterfalls and a gracious host or hostess to assist me. I get goose-bumps as I see the circular inner courtyard with its meditation garden, koi ponds and pergola. The deck is shaped like the yin-yang symbol of balance and the air is fragranced by the sweet smell of incense. The outer hallways lead to offices, classrooms and activity areas where healing is taking place. The three main sections for mind, body, & spirit care are staffed with compassionate, competent individuals who thoroughly love working at The Merging Hearts Holistic Center. They are both friends and coworkers happy to be of service to others and happy to receive healthy compensation for their efforts. People come from around the world to be at our Center to receive our healing services, experience spiritual growth, and peacefully rest amid the quiet surroundings. Our Center is seen as a resource for Indigo children and their families as we help the children develop their spiritual gifts. War veterans come to heal from the traumas they have experienced. Those with cancer and other diseases are healed through the use of reiki, vibrational healing, sound and light therapy and other alternative healing methods. I get excited to see this whole scenario in my mind's eye! Can you tell? Can you tell how much thought I have put into the details of the surroundings? I can see the sacred labyrinth beyond the walls of the Center. There are walking paths and meditation gardens near the ponds. I can hear the music. I can smell the flowers and essences of oils. I can see the many colors of the stained glass in the doors. You need to imagine what you want in detail, and Grand Mother Universe will bring it to you.

Everything, yes everything, has its start in thought. We affect our surroundings. In quantum physics we're now finding that the mere act of looking at an object changes its behavior. I don't understand how this happens just like I don't really understand how I can send an email through the ethers to my friend in Canada. But as we learn to harness this power and aim it towards the best in life, we will be empowered beyond our realm of understanding. Those who have mastered the spiritual realm will harness this power faster and with less effort than those who are still learning. But it is available to all. The power is available to anyone and those who use it for the greater good will have much more power than those who use it for selfish and greedy motives. Grand Mother Universe knows the difference in our motives. Those who are working for spiritual elevation of the planet will receive more blessings and assistance than those with selfish intentions. The intentions of your desires make a remarkable difference in the way your desires will show up and how fast they will manifest. Those whose intentions are to make the world a better place will find it easier and faster to create their surroundings in order to help others. Things will happen with ease. When your vibration reaches the levels of unconditional love, you will create things automatically—right in front of your eyes and right in front of others. They will see the power that is available to the truly holy and others will follow you on your path to wholeness. Not because they want things but because they will see your ability to create peace and wholeness and abundance with your thoughts. That is the way of God. That is what Grand Mother Universe is waiting to help you with! It's time to ask for her help! She's been waiting a long time for your requests!

I've included a few lines here to let you talk to Grand Mother Universe. Thank her in advance for the things, people, jobs, events that she is bringing into your life.

Thank you for _____

_____

Thank you for _____

_____

Thank you for _____

_____

As we focus on what we want, we change our experiences. We literally create our world. It may take time before you and I really get the hang of this, but as more and more of us reach enlightenment, we will use this power to create a new world. We will go beyond wishing for personal items, such as a new self-cleaning oven, to more global solutions, like creating workplaces that are fair and enjoyable. We will create a world of peace and abundance so that no one is hungry, no one is alone or afraid, and no one is left feeling less than the powerful children of God that we are. As we move from our victim consciousness to our manifesting consciousness, we will shine our Light on others. We will move from being those who sit back and take what life gives us to becoming wonderful people of creation, bringing love, laughter and abundance into our lives and into the lives of others. We've created the mess we're in with our "stinkin' thinkin'" but we didn't know we were doing it. So let's now create a different world for ourselves—a world of peace and abundance and kindness. Join me as we awaken to the world of illusion...a wonderful world that we create with our thoughts.

Let's make this third Unity principle more personal: **I create my experiences with the activity of my mind. Everything has its start in my thoughts.**

Fourth Unity Principle

PRAYER IS CREATIVE THINKING THAT HEIGHTENS THE CONNECTION WITH GOD-MIND AND THEREFORE BRINGS FORTH WISDOM, HEALING, PROSPERITY AND EVERYTHING GOOD.

PRAYER IS THE CONNECTION YOU have with God. It the open communication you have with the Divine Source. You can ask questions of the Universal Intelligence for guidance with the incidentals of your daily life and with the bigger questions of your purpose or mission in life. Prayer is the act of going to that quiet place within and connecting to our indwelling Spirit, that Spark of the Divine that exists inside. Prayer is not asking for presents of a Santa Claus-type God who exists outside of us, nor are we pleading on bended knee for mercy for being a sinner. Know that you are one with God and that God provides for us for our highest good. Prayer is the ongoing conversation that you have with the Spirit world. It is walking through life feeling connected on a constant basis with God and his/her helpers, at one with the Spirit realm.

Your angels and spirit guides are helpers from God. They help bring into existence that which you can perceive with your creative mind. If you can imagine yourself being peaceful, being healthy, having prosperity, being wise or anything else good, the spirit realm will co-create that with you. In our Sunday morning spiritual discussion group called Enlightened Beings, we have described prayer as the asking of God, while meditation as the listening to God. Both are parts of the ongoing conversation that exist between you and God as you go about your day. There is no need to wait until we are in church or in our meditation room to talk to God. We can express our gratitude, make our requests and share our concerns at any time. We can listen for God's answers during quiet times of meditation or contemplation, but there are other ways to get your messages from God. You may have spirit guides or angels who bring information your way through a friend, brochure, or email. You may get your answers through journaling or automatic writing. Messages may come to you as you paint or compose, play an instrument or arrange flowers. Be aware of your inner messages when you are quietly reading or taking a walk in nature. When you are peacefully scrapbooking or creating a lovely meal, an inner voice may just whisper the answer to your question or reveal your internal wisdom. Pay attention to that gut feeling. Let your intuition guide you. Just remember to listen to it. And then don't discount it. I so often would just brush a message aside, saying that I had thought it up. Messages from God or from the guides and angels feel different. You'll start to learn the difference between *your* thoughts, the ones you or your ego create, from the ideas or answers brought from the spiritual world. Your ego will create doubt and even tease you about relying on your intuition and messages, but trust yourself to know the difference.

Trust that you have the ability to communicate with the spiritual world. You do have that ability. We all do. It's just that no one has told you that before. Trust the fact that you can receive guidance from the Divine. It's then your part to act on it, or not. This is where free will comes in to play. You may be told to take a certain job, drive a certain road, or help a certain person, but it is your free will on whether you will listen to your internal spiritual voice or discard it in favor of your ego's voice. Communication with God is natural. We were created to have a two-way conversation with Spirit all the time. We're wired that way. But if you don't believe it or have the internal phone turned off, you'll never receive the many messages of guidance and love that the Holy Spirit is sending you.

When dealing with issues that are a result of your abuse, ask God for the gentle knowing that you are safe and secure and that no further harm will come to you. Ask your guardian angels and spirit guides to reveal themselves to you. Ask your angels and spirit guides to speak to you. We are each assigned many spiritual helpers who are along with us on this journey. They are waiting to help us. Some may come for a certain period in our life, while others are assigned to us for the duration of our journey. But we must ask for their help. Angels and spirit guides can really only help us when we ask for their assistance. They are not to interfere with our lives. They may protect us from accidents or guide certain people or information into our lives, but we have the final say as to the actions we take and the information that we use or discard. I have recently become aware of my guardian angel, a powerful female entity named Myrrnah, who is a glowing being with hair of gold and magnificent white wings. She is huge, and I do mean huge! Myrrnah shows up quickly when asked and then grows upward like Jack and the Beanstalk until all I can see of her is the gentle folds of her voluminous, glowing skirt. She is powerful and strong with a gentle heart and a fierce protective nature. I ask her to surround me with her wings and to envelop me, my house, my car and my loved ones with her aura of protection. My constant spirit guide is Daniel, a beautiful young twenty-something male with curly, brown hair and an angelic face. When I call his name, he always answers, "Yes, my sweet!" How cute is that! When he first revealed himself to me during an angel workshop, I kind of cringed a bit at his name. I have a deck of Angel Cards by Doreen Virtue, PhD, called *Messages from Your Angels*, that I refer to quite often for comfort and guidance. There is a card in that deck for the angel Daniel. On that card he says, "I am the Angel of Marriage, and I am assisting you right now." Well, I've been married and divorced twice before and I really don't want to be married again. I'm very happy with my relationship with Wayne and we have agreed that marriage is not the route we want to follow. We're very happy with our commitment to each other and the living arrangements we have created together. When I heard that my guide's name was Daniel, I thought he was going to try to marry me off to someone! So, I doubted his name and shunned his presence. But he kept showing up and calling me 'My sweet!" So one day I hesitantly looked at the accompanying booklet that comes with the deck of angel cards. The booklet gives a longer description of each angel and what they are helping you with. It was there that I found some comforting and inspiring words. In the first paragraph on Daniel's page it reads,

> The first area that I am helping you with is healing any past wounds related to marriage. In quiet moments, I ask that you be willing to release to me any pain associated with your parents. I ask that you breathe out any negative feelings that you may have about marriage, which stem from your childhood experiences.

Well, I'll be! Isn't that just the healing that I need! I have all kinds of negative feelings about marriage because of my parents. This helped me recognize and heal the lingering pessimistic thoughts and emotions I had toward marriage in general and my folks in particular. The second paragraph of the Daniel page states,

> Next, I put my hand upon your heart and ask you to breathe in and out deeply. I now ask that you be willing to release old pain or anger toward your first love. As you release these toxins from your heart, I next ask you to exhale old pain toward all of your past lovers. Allow me to clear your heart of old wounds so that you can enjoy a happy marriage rooted in the

present. We must release the past to avoid replicating old, painful experiences. I am here to free your heart so that it can fully love…within a blissful marriage.

From this reading I uncovered many negative feelings and thoughts I still had about my own marriages. Daniel helped me to identify and release the anger that I still held onto at my second husband. I didn't realize that I still harbored resentment towards him for cheating on me and ruining our chances of adopting a child. Because that anger was revealed to me, I worked on forgiving him through prayer, and through techniques taught by Colin Tipping on *Radical Forgiveness* and through Dr. Len and his book, *Zero Limits*. Those feelings of anger and resentment, that I didn't realize were even there, are now gone and are replaced with a compassion for him and gratitude for the part he played in my development. I'm still not sure if my spirit guide, Daniel, is the same Angel of Marriage Daniel in Doreen's card deck, but it really doesn't matter. My Daniel is there for me and answers prayers for me and comforts me at any time. Through the angel card he led me to unearth some buried resentments and release them. Since it centered on marriage, it would have been very easy for me to discount the Angel Card Daniel and pooh-pooh that the message was for me. But I was brave enough and humble enough to take a look at the entire reading and find the message that was in it for me.

Releasing the old resentments has allowed me to deepen my relationship with Wayne. I could see how past feelings of betrayal and anger were flowing forward onto my current relationship and coloring it wrongfully. I found I was hyper-vigilant towards Wayne about where he was and what he was doing. Now, when I get a feeling of fear that Wayne might start cheating on me or is not being honest about his activities, I ask myself if there is really anything in his behavior that is dishonest or even shows a hint of untrustworthiness, or am I allowing the fear of betrayal from my past to color my current reality. From what I've learned from *A Course in Miracles*, it is at this time when I ask for Divine intervention. I ask for Spirit to enter in this holy instant and change my thoughts. Instead of jumping to conclusions, I allow for the Truth to be revealed to me. I'm more at ease now. I don't question as much. I enjoy my life more. And by the way, Wayne is always where he says he is and always calls when plans change or he's going to be late. He really gives me no reason to think he's being unfaithful, but my past can project its unsavory stench on my present moment. It is my job to seek assistance in viewing the present with fresh eyes and to enjoy the flavor of the present moment.

Just a note: Since writing this segment in 2008, our relationship has changed. Wayne and I were wed October 16, 2010 and I am enjoying a wonderful marriage to this handsome, supportive man. As each of us grew spiritually, our fears of marriage faded away and we wanted to be a committed family unit. It surprised us! We really never thought we would get married but I'm certainly glad we did!

Wedding Day, October 16, 2010

Let me share a story about my spirit guide Daniel. One day after an Enlightened Beings session, Wayne and I stopped at the grocery store to pick up some items. As we were walking out of the store and into the parking lot, a beautiful young man with brown curly hair ran past us to his car that was parked beside ours. He looked exactly like Daniel! He looked so much like him that I was speechless—a big statement for a talker like me. Wayne was pushing the grocery cart and I started hitting him on the arm. My mouth was wide open and my eyes were bulging as I pointed to the young man. "What?" Wayne said. "That's him! That young man looks just like Daniel." I watched as the young man got into his beat up ole clunker and rode off. I was in awe of the likeness of this beautiful young man to the image I see of my angel, Daniel. I didn't even help put the groceries in the back of the SUV as I just stood there and stared at the car driving away. I later revealed this incident to Laura Lyn, our Angel Reader, and she giggled and said that "Yes, our guides often play games with us and manifest right in front of us!" Well, that floored me! I didn't know they would do that, or even that they could do that!

So, find out who your angels and guides are and talk to them. Pray to God and his spiritual assistants. Bring your gratitude to the Source of all creation. Ask for things you want and need and then ask that they be given to you if they are for your highest good. Sometimes we may ask for a resolution to a situation and it doesn't come. In that case, we often are in the process of learning an important life lesson during this journey. Or maybe we don't really believe they will appear or that we are not worthy of receiving. When things are rough or you're feeling especially lonely or sad, and your requests continue to go unanswered, go within and ask what lesson you are to learn from this situation. Ask that the wisdom that comes from experiencing this situation be revealed to you so that you may know the reason for your grief, suffering or anger. Use prayer to lighten the load and gain inner wisdom.

An important part of prayer is visualization. You must vividly see yourself in the circumstance of having that situation, receiving a particular item, achieving that goal or being somewhere in particular.

With your eyes closed, imagine what it feels like to hold the item that you desire. What does it feel like to reach that goal? Who is around and what are they saying to you? Imagine yourself as healthy and strong! What are the smells and sights of that place you want to visit or live in? What does it feel like to be calm and powerful? There are many books and videos out now for co-creating your reality with God. Use the instructions available from *The Secret* and the Law of Attraction to achieve the kind of life you want. It can help you get an A on your essay for your grad class or help bring about peace within your community. Prayer can bring you material goods, nurturing relationships, a healthy mind and body, and inner wisdom…whatever you want. But you must first ask. You must make it known to God and the spirit realm what your heart desires and then believe that it is coming to you. Expect it to happen. And it will! Prayer brings you closer to the Divine. It keeps the lines of communication open between you and God. He/She is available to help you with wise solutions to your problems, with loving guidance on how to handle situations, or with kind advice on settling your internal chaos. Communicate through prayer with God and you'll learn to live your life with ease.

For us abuse victims, we need to pray to God for the release of negative emotions. Pray for healing—emotional healing, psychological healing and physical healing. All parts of us were damaged by the sexual abuse and we can heal all parts of us with the help of Spirit. Ask God that the fear that grips you when starting a new relationship or starting to make love be released so that the true spirit of your divine feminine is brought forth into your life. Ask that the wee, little you inside your body be healed of its feeling of inferiority and unworthiness so that you can go out and be the best you. Ask for help in healing the inner child who is scared and needy. Ask for help in seeing your own Divine Light. Ask for peace and calmness, both in your inner world and your outer world. Ask that your relationships be nurturing and prosperous. And when you ask for all of this, expect it to happen. Watch for it to happen. Look for the changes you see in yourself and in others' behavior. Become the observer as your life changes before your eyes. Be amazed at the wonderful things that happen to you. Keep a journal of the changes you see and the wonderful things, people and events that show up in your life, even the little things. When we become aware of the results, the angels and guides know we're paying attention and will bring us more and more success. Notice the synchronicities. There's a great little book called *When God Winks, How the Power of Coincidence Guides Your Life* by Squire Rushnell. Thank God and your angels and guides for the work they have done in bringing these things to pass. Thank them for all the work they are doing currently to bring additional wonderful things, relationships and situations to your journey. Develop your awareness to the point that you are always expecting something good to show up. As Dr. Joe Dispenza says in the movie *What the Bleep Do We Know?!*:

> I'm taking this time to create my day and I'm affecting the quantum field. Now if (it) is in fact the observer's watching me the whole time that I'm doing this and there is a spiritual aspect to myself, then show me a sign today that you paid attention to any one of these things that I created, and bring them in a way that I won't expect, so I'm surprised at my ability to be able to experience these things. And make it so that I have no doubt that it has come from you, and so I live my life, in a sense, all day long thinking about being a genius or thinking about being the glory and the power of God or thinking about being unconditional love.

Start living within the spirit realm on a daily, minute-to-minute basis. We are in the thick of the spirit realm, not disconnected and apart from it. Prayer can help release the anxiety and the negative vibes that live within us caused by our abuse. When we realize that all things are possible, and that we merely need to ask for healing or money or wisdom, we will start living in the moment and realizing our dreams of peacefulness and inner emotional health. If you are about to go into a stressful meeting at work or must be around unsupportive family members, breathe deeply and ask that your angels and spirit guides surround you and protect you. Ask that your inner Spirit be present, the Spirit that will make you calm and strong. Not verbally aggressive or standoffish strong, but to carry you throughout the meeting or family gathering in love.

Here's our fourth Unity principle stated as a personal affirmation: **My prayers are creative thoughts that heighten the connection with the Divine. They therefore bring forth wisdom, healing, prosperity and everything good.**

Fifth Unity Principle

Knowing and understanding the Law of Life, also called TRUTH, is not enough. We must live the truth we know.

The Law of Life is simply that we are all one, that we are all connected in the web of life. What we do to another, we do to ourselves, to every other human and to our environment. We are inherently connected to each other, to every other living thing, to Mother Earth and to Spirit. Every thought affects your surroundings. Every word spoken affects the atmosphere. Every action sends ripples out in the never-ending pool of frequencies. Everything you do either increases the vibration of your surroundings or decreases the vibration of your surroundings. We are all connected in a complex network of energy.

If we cheat someone, we are essentially cheating ourselves. If we hurt someone's feelings, that energy will return to us and our feelings will be hurt. If we damage relationships by lying, our other relationships will be damaged. The effect may not be immediate in some cases, but our thoughts, words and actions affect everything and everyone else. The Biblical message, "as ye sow, so shall ye reap," is this fundamental Law of the Universe. If you think, speak or act in selfish, mean, or dishonest ways, you are literally affecting the vibes around you, sending negatives air waves throughout the world. And those same negative vibes are what you will attract back to you.

If you give kindness, you'll get kindness. If you give forgiveness, you are sending positive frequencies into the airwaves and people will be kinder to you. If you bring peace into situations, you'll live in a more harmonious place. If you give of your resources, your wealth will be replenished many times over. This is not new information to anyone. But what we do not realize is the extent of our power in transforming our surroundings. This power to affect our environment is real. It is the TRUTH, with capital letters! Living your life everyday in loving ways will bring you a loving world. In your quest for peace and happiness, follow Gandhi's words, "You must be the change you want to see in the world."

Victims of abuse often behave within a fearful paradigm. If you continue to act in this way, you are sending out vibrations of fear, and you can only receive back more fearful situations in your life. When you learn to trust that God is here and will protect you, you will operate differently in the world. I often am fearful that there is not enough money to pay the bills. I am learning that God will provide to the extent that I think he will provide. If I believe in lack, that is what I will get back. If I believe there will be just enough to eke by, that's what will transpire. If I believe there is an abundance of money for me to have, then I will receive more than enough to take care of myself and others. You can change your life by changing your thoughts and actions.

Since everything is connected, the emotion I project out to the world, in thoughts, actions or words, will return back to me again and again. What I believe in my core is the hologram I create for my reality. If I believe the world is a scary place, I will attract people and events that make that belief true. If I believe the world is a safe place, I will attract (create) the people and events that produce a safe environment. We are all connected by a web of consciousness and as we raise our frequency, our internal vibration, from fear and shame to love and compassion, we affect the entire world. Our vibration radiates out from us and affects the environment. We all know of a person that negatively affects the vibe of a place as soon as he or she walks in the room. You can feel the coolness, the tension within the room. Well, the opposite is true as well. We can affect a room with our positive vibe. We can cause a rise in the vibration of a private conversation, a meeting at the office, or a volatile situation in a bar. As you are working to heal yourself, know that you are also healing the world. You're causing your frequency to increase which means your Light burns a little brighter. Your aura interacts with the auras of others and hence, increases their vibration. You'll feel the difference. Others will feel the difference. It's subtle, hard to put into words, but it can be felt. It's delicate, yet powerful.

Dr. Wayne Dyer describes this power of thought in his wonderful book, *The Power of Intention*. He looks at intention as "a field of energy you can access to begin co-creating your life." He summarizes the work of scientist Dr. David Hawkins by saying that "In essence, every single person as well as large groups of people can be calibrated for their energy levels." I believe that people who have been sexually abused calibrate at much lower energy levels. Dr. Hawkins has developed a "Map of Consciousness" in his book *Power vs Force*. This Map of Consciousness (Pg 68-69) lists the "calibrated levels that correlate with specific processes of consciousness – emotions, perceptions, or attitudes, worldviews and spiritual beliefs." (Pg 67) In other words, he has found the vibrational frequency of various emotions within the human experience. The frequencies are logged in a range from 1 to 1000. People who are experiencing the emotions of shame and guilt vibrate at the lowest levels on the chart, between 20 and 30. Fear measures in at 100. If the sexual abuse we experienced has made us exist at these low vibrational frequencies, we can never experience the true joy of life and the happiness of love that measure in the 500-540 range. Our perpetrators may have stuffed us into the bottom of the frequency barrel, but we certainly do not have to stay there. It is our duty to take responsibility for our life and begin increasing our vibrational frequency and move up the Map of Consciousness.

Dr. Hawkins states, "The critical response point in the scale of consciousness calibrates at level 200, which is the level associated with integrity and courage…This is the balance point between weak and strong attractors, between negative and positive influence." You can raise your frequency to higher levels of happiness by changing your thoughts and living your life in accordance with the truth of who you are. You are a vibrating energy field created by God. You affect your surroundings and your future by the thoughts you think, the actions you perform, and the words you speak. Become aware of your thought patterns and be diligent about changing your patterns of thinking. Live your life as a powerful creation of God. Together, you and God can get you un-stuck from your current level of performing and thinking. There is definite hope for changing your patterns. You can regain your innate sense of power and intention through continued use of the methods described in this book. You can live a life that is harmonious and meaningful, and leave the anxiety and despair behind.

So now that you know this Law of Life, the concept that we are all connected and influenced by each other, you must live it. It's not good enough just to intellectually understand it, you must consciously live knowing that we are all energetically joined. You must actively work at raising your own vibration. You must consciously make the decision to raise your frequency before a conversation or during an argument. You can ask your Higher Self to see the best in the person in front of you and ask for Divine Guidance in your words and actions. Instead of acting out of a place of fear, come from a place of love. Don't react with quick judgments and a sharp tongue. Breathe and ask for guidance. Am I reacting to past hurts? Respond in a slow, easy cadence while trying to see the other person's Spark of Divinity. Speak from your heart more and your head less.

Here's a more personal statement of the fifth Unity principle: **I know and understand the Law of Life, that everything is connected through frequencies. But knowing this TRUTH is not enough. I must live the truth I know and consciously raise my vibration from fear, anger and shame to love.**

Summary of Unity Principles

Let's make a quick summary of these wonderful Unity Principles.

1. **God is absolute good and everywhere present.** If I truly believe and know that God is good then I know that God is always taking care of me in the best way possible. That's for now while on this planet Earth and when I die. He/She only wants the best for me in this life… and when this life is over. I don't have to live in fear that I'm going to hell for not believing a certain philosophy, nor for cutting my hair, nor for eating on a Sabbath day. Believe that God is sending you love and care and abundance. Open your arms to his love. Open your arms to her gifts. Open your heart and accept the joyous, wondrous love from the Divine. It is yours…it's waiting for you to open your arms and heart. Accept the love you feel around you. Welcome the joy that comes from living within this truth…that God is good and everywhere present.

Imagine that you are wading through an ocean of love. Visualize yourself walking through a mystical cloud of love that surrounds you with eternal warmth and care, that the air you breathe is filled with magic and wonder. Feel the spiritual aura of God around you.

No matter where you are…at home, at the office, at the beach, in the woods, in your car, in the mall, in Starbucks, in line at the unemployment office, in your bathtub, in your bed. Feel the wonder of a loving God surround you. Imagine yourself walking through a thick mist and be in awe of the beauty and wonder of all of life's creations. Recognize that the love of God exists inside you and inside each and every thing that is here on Earth. When you start seeing God in everyone and everything, the magic will start to happen! Be the observer and look at everything in a new way. Tell yourself: I am loved by God! Everything is filled with the wonder of God! Everyone is filled with the love of God! All is good! Good things are coming to me now! God is good and everywhere present.

2. **We have a spark of divinity within. Our very essence is of God and we are therefore inherently good**. This was the most powerful principle for me as far as changing the way I felt about myself. Knowing that at my core I had a spark of God within me was the concept that had the most impact on my healing. Between the teachings of original sin from the Baptist church and the emotional damage done by my father's abuse, I had a strong sense of being worthless or not good enough. I didn't really *think* it was true but the doubt was always there. Am I okay? Am I as good as everyone else? I had always felt a sense of incompleteness, a feeling that I was different and missing something that everyone else had. Even with my college degrees and noted accomplishments there was still an internal nagging emptiness that made me feel inadequate or flawed, not quite as good as everyone else.

When I internalized the concept that I have a spark of divinity within me, I felt whole. I felt okay. I felt on an equal footing with everyone else. I didn't have an internal flaw after all. I felt sure that I was made of goodness. Say this out loud right now, "I have a spark of Divinity within me!" Listen to your internal talk. Does your ego voice drown your spirit voice out? Or do you feel the spark within your sacred heart? Picture that small flame inside you and imagine it growing larger and larger. It is always burning. It has always been there. And now as you recognize it and acknowledge your spark of Divinity, it will grow and become more powerful! But it is not enough to just *know* it and *understand* that you have a spark of Divinity within you. Principle number 5 states that you must *live* this truth. Live your life as if you have a Divine spark within you! Present yourself to others that you are a Divine child of God. Make decisions about how to take care of yourself as if you are a Divine spark. Set healthy boundaries with folks on how a Divine creation of God should be treated. This is not to say that you should become a diva or a bitch, but that you should take pride in the Divine creature that you are. When I presented myself to others as a Divine spark, rather than a damaged piece of goods, people treated me differently. When I believed myself that I was a Divine creation, I talked to myself better, fed myself better, treated myself better. Say it again, "I have a spark of Divinity within me!" Whenever you are feeling down on yourself, feeling nervous before a corporate presentation or meeting your mother-in-law, say "I am a Divine creation of God!" Build true confidence in yourself by reminding yourself daily of your inherent goodness. Don't just try to be good. Say to yourself, "I am a good person!" and "I am a kind person." Start your sentences with "I am" and they will be much more powerful.

I would often do good things or be kind to folks in hopes that they would tell me that I was good or kind. And no matter how many times I heard it, I still didn't believe it or know it in my heart. I didn't feel it inside. I still felt inadequate. When I started telling myself, "I am a good person" and "I am a kind person," it started to stick! I had to convince me that I was okay. It had to be my voice that really changed the way I thought about myself. And when I realized that I had a spark of divinity within me, I knew that at my core I was okay. I was adequate, in fact more than adequate. I was a wonderful creation of God!

I might still get a little nervous about giving a presentation or meeting someone of importance, but it is just a slight case of butterflies and not the dread that came before, wondering if I would make a mistake or be rejected by the person. I present myself as a wonderful child of God who is meeting another wonderful child of God! We must live the truth we know! So, even if you don't quite believe it fully, live your life *as if* you have a spark of Divinity within you!

3. **We create our experiences by the activity of our minds. Everything has its start in thought.** The process of living this principle must be the growing awareness of what is going on in your head. Your increased awareness of your inner self-talk will allow you to change the thoughts that are flowing through your head. As you listen to and stop the negative self-talk, you will literally change your life! When you hear yourself say, "I'll never find someone to love," say "Stop! Erase that!" Replace it with "I am lovable and my partner is coming to me now!" You must literally change what is playing on your internal CD. When the internal CD is saying, "Nothing ever goes my way!" say "Stop! Erase that!" Change your inner dialogue to "God loves me and is sending wonderful people and events into my life!" I have many different affirmations taped to my computer, my refrigerator, my dashboard, my bathroom mirror…anywhere that I happen to spend time that will remind me that I am my thoughts. These little slips of paper bring me back to awareness of who I really am and that I am in charge of my life. I am in charge of whom I bring into my life from now on. I am in charge of how I think about situations and people that enter my life. Now that you know and understand this important Law of Life, put your mind to work for you to create the life you want to live. We can all put our minds to work for the good of all. Together we can create a world of peace and harmony, abundance and trust. We can change our thoughts and create a wonderful world.

4. **Prayer is creative thinking that heightens the connection with God-Mind and therefore brings forth wisdom, healing, prosperity, and everything good.** Living this principle is very similar to the principle above, but its difference is subtle and very important. Principle 3 to me is about the attitude I have about the world around me. I can view a situation as miserable or disgusting, or I can view it as a learning experience and look for the good in it. It's how I interpret a situation that gives it meaning. I can change my thoughts in order to change my world.

Principle 4 is more about strengthening the bond between me and God. I can co-create with Spirit all of the things I desire, as long as they are for the highest good for everyone concerned. Using prayer to ask for guidance from God, I listen quietly for God's messages. I strengthen my connection with God in the same way I strengthen my connection with friends and family. I communicate and spend time with them. I share concerns, ask for guidance, and listen to the advice or comments they give. I do the same with Spirit. I communicate and spend time in the presence of God. This will raise my vibrational frequency allowing me to attract the wisdom, love, healing and prosperity that I deserve.

But here's where it has always been a little hard for me. I have a lot of trouble asking for help. Whether it's from Wayne, a girlfriend or a coworker, I have trouble asking for assistance or advice. So asking for help from God was never easy! I felt I had to be self-sufficient at everything and be all-knowing of everything. There's that need to be perfect again and the fear of showing that I'm inadequate rears its ugly head again. It's like having a million lifelines on the old TV show "Who Wants to be a Millionaire" and never using any of them, because someone will find out I don't know the answer! Use the lifelines that God has given you and receive the answers you need for the life that you want.

I'm really learning to use the simple phrase "Let Go, and Let God." That has been a very big lesson for me to trust in the Holy Spirit that exists within me and to talk to it. Rely on the good information and guidance that is there for your assistance. Talk to God. Listen for the answers. Ask Spirit to help you make the smallest of choices along with the really big decisions. We must live the TRUTH we know. Know that God is within you and wants your best and will assist you in healing your body, gaining prosperity, and bringing forth your inner wisdom. Strengthen your connection with God by using your lifelines. Every day. All day. Feel connected to God at all times. Spirit is always there, always around us. Take part in this Divine conversation and feel the goodness of God erase your feelings of inadequacy. Ask God to help you rid yourself of the fear of intimacy. Talk to God about the inner child who is still afraid of the world. Ask for assistance in your emotional, physical, and psychological healing. It will be different for everyone. What I needed to do for my mental health may not work for anyone else. The technique or activity that will help you heal an inner wound may sound strange to someone else, but it may be exactly what you need to mend a broken heart.

One time I was feeling very depressed and couldn't really put a finger on what was causing the sadness and despair. I asked my inner child, Little Jeanne, what she needed right then to be happy. I suddenly saw a vision of a coloring book and a big box of 64 Crayola crayons in my head. She wanted to color! It sounded silly, but my counselor often told me to listen to my inner child. So, I went to the store and let my inner child choose a coloring book. The store was out of Crayola crayons so I picked up a small box of waxy crayons from another company. This will do, I told myself.

"AAAAAAAAAAAAAAAAAAAAAAAAAAAH!" I heard this screeching yell inside my head! My inner child was throwing a tantrum! "I want the big box, the green and gold box!" I heard. Well, luckily, I listened to that voice in my head, set down the small box of waxy crayons and went to another store. I found the perfect box of 64 Crayola crayons and headed home. I allowed myself to sit down with my new coloring book and my shiny green and gold box of 64 Crayola crayons and become quiet. I then told Little Jeanne that these were her new toys and she was allowed to come out and play with them. It wasn't long before I opened the coloring book and started coloring.

My heart filled with joy each time I opened the lid on the Crayola box and looked at all the wonderful pointed color sticks! I colored a couple of pictures that day and then again on a few more days. The healing that took place was wonderful. I honored my inner child by allowing her to feel special and acknowledged. I have no idea why that particular activity changed me. I don't know what wound it helped heal, but it healed something. I listened to God, to that spark of Divinity within me, and followed the guidance I was given – to go get some crayons and a coloring book. This simple and inexpensive activity may only be helpful for me, but I got the message from within and honored that message. You must ask for guidance for your own healing and listen for the answers. Don't discount the answers you get. Don't make fun of them. Honor them. They may appear silly or feel like nonsense, but it's what your inner child, your soul, needs in order to heal. Take it seriously as you hear these messages. Trust your intuition. If your inner child wants to play on a swing set, squish some Playdoh, or just sift sand through her fingers, let yourself indulge in these private inner moments with God that will restore your mental and emotional health.

Ask. Listen. Do.

Let Spirit help you on your journey of recovery. God wants you to be happy with your outer world and your inner world. Ask for help, listen to the suggestions, and do what is offered. Your spirit will sing as the inner connection to Spirit grows.

5. **Knowing and understanding the Law of Life, also called TRUTH, is not enough. We must live the truth we know.** The Law of Life is that everything is connected in a complex network of energy. You now know that:

- What you **think** affects your future.
- What you **say** sends out vibrational messages to the Universe about what you expect your life to be.
- What you **do** to others will be done to you.

But knowing and understanding this isn't good enough. You must live your life in ways that show you know the truth of how the universe works. You must act responsibly towards yourself. Find your place on the Map of Consciousness and set your intention to raise your level. Have hope that you can raise above your current status on the chart through counseling and by using the techniques I mention in the book. When you ask for Divine guidance and dwell in a space of love, your healing will take place. You will start your climb to living in Love.

TO FINISH THIS CHAPTER, HERE ARE THE FIVE UNITY PRINCIPLES WRITTEN AS PERSONAL AFFIRMATIONS:

1. God is absolute good. God is present with me everywhere I go.
2. I have a Spark of Divinity within me. My very essence is of God and therefore, I am inherently good and worthwhile!
3. I create my experiences with the activity of my mind. Everything has its start in my thoughts.
4. My prayers are creative thoughts that heighten the connection with the Divine. They therefore bring forth wisdom, healing, prosperity and everything good to me.
5. I know and understand the Law of Life, that everything is connected through frequencies. But knowing this TRUTH is not enough. I must live the truth I know and consciously raise my vibration from shame, fear and anger to compassion, forgiveness and love.

Put these principles into action. Put them to work for you. Do them and watch your anxiety decrease and your joy increase. Gaze at your life as an observer while the sadness and depression leave and the happiness and serenity come into your awareness. It is really possible to rid yourself of the damaging scars that sexual abuse can bring. I did it, and so can you. Believe that it can happen for you. Practice these principles every day, but especially on the rough days. That's when I really needed them. On the tough days when I would forget that God was good and that I had a spark of Divinity within me, I needed the constant reminders. When I was sad and lonely, I needed the prompts that my thoughts were creating my reality. When I was struggling, I needed a cue to quit going it alone and start using prayer and talk to Spirit for comfort and guidance. Say these Unity principles out loud. Write them down. Stick them on your kitchen cupboards. They've made a wonderful difference in my life and I'm sure they will help you rise above the damages done by your abuser. As your Divinity becomes more aware to you, you'll raise your vibrational frequency and you'll start attracting the serenity and harmonious lifestyle you so desire.

Namaste—The Divine in me sees the Divine in you!

Please visit the Unity website for more information about this spiritual organization at www.unity.org.

Since its inception in 1924, Unity's publication, The *Daily Word*, has provided people of all faiths with positive words of truth and inspiration. You can sign up for daily affirmations by going to www.dailyword.com.

Part V:
Forgiveness

Three Levels of Forgiveness

November 6, 2008 was an unseasonably warm 70 degrees for this late in the year in Ohio. My friend Teresa called and we went for a bike ride along the scenic Erie Canal towpath trail here in northeast Ohio. We started out in Massillon and rode for about an hour north towards the village of Canal Fulton. Teresa knew I was writing this book and asked for more details about it. I told her about my childhood experiences of abuse, how spirituality helped me heal, and how the book was to help others heal from this same horrible experience. She asked me how I could possibly forgive such horrendous behavior by my father. I thought a moment and these thoughts came to my mind. I had never thought of it in this way before, but I heard a voice telling me that forgiveness comes in levels. I explained the three levels of forgiveness to her as we rode our bikes amid the beautiful fall leaves and warm sunshine. I had never thought about the forgiveness being in levels before, but the divine thoughts came into my head as I rode along the Erie Canal path and spoke the ideas aloud to my friend, Teresa. I'd like to share them here with you.

First Level of Forgiveness

THE FIRST LEVEL OF FORGIVENESS for me was giving up the anger. In my early thirties, the flashbacks of the abuse started surfacing and I was devastated. I was overridden with fear, totally immobilized at times with fright. In those early stages when I was having a flashback, it felt like I was being abused right then, right there. The emotions that flooded my body and my mind were tremendously powerful—erasing all sense of the current moment—the room, the building, the people around me, the safe surroundings were all gone, replaced by the feeling of being a little girl being brutally attacked and horrendously violated. I would be crying, hyperventilating, screaming out. This would all be happening to me while having the first flashbacks.

Once I was able to return to the present moment and realize I was safe in my own home, the rage would start growing in me. Raging, venomous thoughts filled my waking moments. My mind and heart were filled with thoughts like:

- How dare you?
- How dare you do such things to me!
- What right did you have to make me do those things?!

- What right did you have to touch me in those ways?!
- You ruined my childhood!
- You stole my innocence!
- I'm your daughter! How could you do this to me?
- You fucking bastard!
- You greedy son-of-a-bitch!
- You selfish asshole!
- How could you do this to me?!
- What the hell's wrong with you?

The angry thoughts filled with expletives and never-ending questions consumed me. The anger grew inside me. It grew and became so immense, so intense, that I was afraid to let it out. I was afraid that if I let one little part of that rage seep out, it would explode and I would never be able to shut it off. I was afraid I would hurt someone or hurt myself.

But more than anything I was afraid I would go crazy. I was afraid the rage would take over my being and I would never return again.

In group therapy we talked about our anger and pent up rage and the need to release it. I stated many times that I was too afraid to release the anger. I felt that if I let it surface it would engulf me and I would never be sane again. The feelings of anger were that strong that I felt they would take over my being and I would be lost forever in a constant state of rage. I was afraid I would morph into this hideous, uncontrollable beast that spewed anger and violence onto everything around me. My group counselor said she had heard that fear before from many others and assured me that they had felt their rage, released it little by little, and had survived. She was certain I would be okay. But I wasn't so sure. She promised that I would not lose myself in the rage. She promised I would not go crazy. She promised I would not go insane.

The counselor taught us how to let out our rage in small doses in safe private surroundings. After months and months of hearing this from my counselor and the women in my group counseling, I finally trusted them enough. I took their advice and allowed myself to experience the rage in small time frames. One of the methods we were taught was to use a tennis racket to let out our anger on the bed. So, bravely one day, I got my tennis racket and started hitting the bed, feeling silly at first and doubting that this would really work. At first I was just tapping the bed with the racket and then hitting it a little harder. I had been advised to talk to my Dad while I was doing this. I began talking to my Dad as if he were standing in the room with me. The anger surfaced and I started hitting the bed harder and harder, sometimes using two hands on the racket and slamming it on the bed. (Note: Be careful of ceiling fans and overhead lights when doing this!) My normal tone of voice became agitated and loud and soon I was screaming out all the things that I wanted to say to my Dad and to my Mom. The physical act of beating something released the pent up memories on a cellular level. With each slam of the racket and with each scream of rage, bits of the negative energy that had been repressed inside my body for so long were released forever. I screamed at the top of my voice and shouted angry, violent statements at both parents. I made demands as to why you (Dad) did this to me and why you (Mom) didn't protect me. The screaming was filled with such foul language that I would never repeat it in front of anyone.

Sometimes there would be no words. There would just be these loud shrieks of grief or low mournful wailings come out of me. It didn't matter. I was releasing repressed emotions from my psyche and from my body. It had to get out of me somehow.

During these sessions, I would often scream about the things I wanted to do to my Dad in retaliation. I wanted to publicly humiliate him and hang him naked from a tree for the world to see. And while he hung there, I would cut off his cock and stick it in his mouth—a fitting retribution, I thought, for all the oral sex he made me perform on him.

These screaming, tennis racket sessions would always start out mild with me barely talking to him. But as the anger surfaced, I would pound harder and scream louder and vent the things that I wanted to say to my Dad. These sessions would last anywhere from 20 min to an hour and I eventually would collapse into a sobbing heap, exhausted and weak. The process was draining, to say the least. But it was so therapeutic. I might have swollen puffy eyes for the next few hours, but I always felt somewhat lighter. It was if I had dumped out the grief and rage from one of the big sacks around my neck and let it fall to Mother Earth to be absorbed by her kind and gentle nature.

And most importantly, I didn't go crazy! I didn't lose myself in the rage forever. I found that I could experience the rage, release some of it, and then shut it off. I recouped my sanity, little by little, feeling lighter, less tense, and less sad.

After awhile, I would not feel that intense rage within, but rather I'd feel an underlying nervousness or edginess. I found that I started planning these sessions when I was feeling lots of anxiety. That's when I knew that the anger was rising and that I had to release it. I don't remember how many times I beat my tennis racket on the bed. You do it as many times as you need to release the rage. You may need only a few sessions or you may find that it takes many, many hours to help you let go of the immense storehouse of rage. It doesn't matter. You're releasing the pent up anger and rage that must be let go to find peace. It can't be done with just thinking about it or talking about it. You have to physically "do" something that will release the rage from the physical form. There must be a release of this anger from the cellular memories in your body through some type of physical activity. I highly recommend some type of physical, emotional release. Other forms of physical activity, like running, kick boxing or hitting a punching bag, may help to get rid of the anger and other negative energies inside every cell of your body. I haven't tried these, but the key is to be doing something physically strenuous while shouting at your perpetrator. It's important to let go of this trapped, agitated energy inside your body in order to feel the serenity of your true nature.

Another method I used to release the rage was something I did purely in my imagination. I would imagine my Dad's face being part of a tree trunk. It was as if he was inside the tree and could put his face against the bark until it stuck out, so that just his face would show to the outside. Then, still in my mind, I would pick up a baseball bat and hit his face over and over and over again. I would yell at him as I hit him, screaming all the things I wanted to say to him. His face would eventually become battered and sunken and would eventually fade into the tree. I would then take a mental rest for awhile and resume normal breathing. His face would then reappear on the side of the tree and I would pick up my imaginary bat and start whaling on him again, and then again, and then again, until I was mentally too tired to beat on him anymore. It was somehow my way of punishing him for the damage and torture he had done to me. It was a good method of releasing that negative energy. These methods are good at releasing most of the rage that dwells within you from sexual abuse and there are others that are helpful. But even after many, many of these rage-releasing sessions, there always seemed to be a core sack of anger that I couldn't release through these procedures.

I finally realized that the concept of forgiveness was the act of laying down that final sack of rage and resentment and just letting go of it. Forgiveness wasn't about saying that what happened to me was okay or that it wasn't important. Forgiveness was saying, "You have done enough damage to me already in my life. I no longer will carry around the heavy weight of rage within me and around me. I release you from having any further control over my life. You hurt me before and I no longer will allow you to hurt me again. You no longer have influence on the quality of my life."

Forgiveness was the releasing of the anger and walking away from it, so that I could have a peaceful, creative life. It's not saying that the abuse didn't matter, nor is it saying that the abuse didn't hurt me. It's simply saying I no longer want to hold the negative feelings from that event within me anymore. The anger affects my peace of mind and that's what I want most of all: Peace.

When I was tired of being angry I could finally forgive.

My anger and resentment weren't affecting **him** one tiny bit. I was the one being damaged by the anger that resided within me. It made me high strung. It made me anxious. It made me irritable. It robbed me of good restful sleep and quiet evenings by the fireplace. It took over my peaceful Spirit by claiming that I had a right to be mad! Look what he did to me! How dare you say to forgive him! But as time passed, I finally got tired of being indignant and distant, angry and restless, short-tempered and judgmental. I just wanted to feel peace. That's all.

So when your desire to be peaceful is stronger than your desire to be right, you'll put down that last ugly sack of rage and walk away from it.

There may be days when you pick it back up again and carry it around for a day or two, or twenty, but then you'll realize what you're doing and you'll lay it back down again. You may need to pick up that tennis racket years from now and wail away on your bed again. That's okay! You may want to look inside the bag on some days to revisit old hurts. That's fine. Just close it back up when you're done and walk away. I find that when a new memory surfaces, I'll pick up the sack of rage and carry it around for awhile. It feels good to be angry! It makes me feel powerful! Then it will grow heavy and I'll grow tiresome. I want my peace back. So again, I will lay down the sack of rage and walk away. That's what forgiveness is. You're saying, "I release you (the person or the anger) from being a part of my everyday life. You're no longer needed or wanted or useful. I'm letting you go so that I can live my life wholly and happily. I let go of the hold you have on me. I forgive you and I'm walking away a free person."

Marianne Williamson wrote a book called *A Return to Love*. It explains in easy to understand terms the main tenets of the spiritual text, *A Course in Miracles*. She shows us how to leave fear and anger behind and 'return to love.' Here's her take on forgiveness:

> Forgiveness is a full time job, and sometimes very difficult. Few of us always succeed, yet making the effort is our most noble calling. It is the world's only

real chance to begin again. A radical forgiveness is a complete letting go of the past, in any personal relationship, as well as in any collective drama.

Forgiveness is often a very difficult step for victims of sexual abuse. At one time I felt that forgiveness was letting my dad off the hook. I felt it was like saying "Oh, it wasn't so terrible. It's okay." But forgiveness isn't that, at all. It's about taking care of your well-being. You've had enough time to be angry or resentful. Now it's time to experience peace. If you don't forgive, your perpetrator is still abusing you. You're allowing him/her to influence the quality of your life. It's time to forgive and be at peace.

Ask for assistance from your angels and spirit guides. Ask for Divine intervention. As Gary Zukav states on page 240 of *The Seat of the Soul*:

> Allow yourself to pray. Just as the many times human beings find themselves in circumstances where the hurt of the pain is so great that on their own power they cannot forgive, it is enough that they pray to be given the grace, the perception, the elevated Light that will allow them to forgive.

Forgiveness is about taking care of you. It's about setting down the heavy baggage of anger and feeling lighter and brighter. Allow God to help you forgive, for where there is no forgiveness, there is no peace.

The Second Level of Forgiveness

THE SECOND LEVEL OF FORGIVENESS for me came with a compassion for what it may have been like growing up as my parents. It helped me gain an understanding of possibly why they are the way they are. I know more about my mother than my Dad. She would often share stories of her childhood and early adulthood. So it has been easier for me to empathize with her mindset, motivations and lack of courage. She grew up during the Depression and was one of eight children. Her family was very poor. She only had two dresses to wear during high school and often felt very ugly and inferior to the other girls in her class. Her father was an alcoholic and very abusive to her mother and other members of the family. I heard stories of how he would completely upset the large dining room table at dinner, if something made him angry during the meal, sending food, plates and children scattered across the room. I realized my Mom was probably sexually abused by her father also. Mom displayed almost every one of the signs and symptoms of a sexually-abused person that I learned about in group therapy classes. She fits the part.

She had learned to be submissive and quiet from her family and from the culture of the 1930's and 1940's. The poverty and sexual abuse made her feel inferior and undesirable. There was no money for therapy and society at that time did not advocate for mental health counseling. Along comes my Dad, a dashing young man just home from the military who is friends with her older brother and he starts courting her. She's amazed that this great looking guy wants to marry her. They wed and start a life together. She is happy beyond her wildest dreams. But years later when she finds he is abusing their daughter, her own unresolved issues of powerlessness and unworthiness come back strong. She feels helpless and vulnerable. There's nowhere for her to turn. She can't talk about such issues to anyone. There are no domestic violence shelters to run to. There are no free services for family counseling or legal advice. She has no skills to earn an income and raise her children on her own. She's stuck. She's stuck with her own consuming feelings of fear and inferiority. No employer would ever want a tired housewife as an employee and no man would ever want her again. She's stuck because, in her world, she has no options.

And then there's the fear of him. She knows he is capable of violence. He owns several guns and never wants anyone questioning his authority in his house. He probably threatened to kill her children if she told anyone. He controlled me into silence by threatening to kill my little brothers if I told anyone about the abuse, so I'm sure he used the same manipulative measures on her. Mentally and emotionally, she is incapable of handling the situation she is in. She simply can't deal with it. She goes into denial and pretends it's not happening. She escapes into her private fantasy world where everything is right and calm. She holds on to this idyllic family façade that she presents to the world and hopes the abuse will just go away.

I'm in no way condoning what my mother did. She should have asked for help. She should have left with her children and gone somewhere, anywhere. She should have fought him and stopped him from abusing me. I could never stand by and watch an adult hurt a child, over and over. There's something very wrong with a person who can allow this type of abuse to happen again and again. My forgiveness for her comes from understanding the mental and emotional state of mind she must have been in to allow this to go on in her home. There's a level of mental illness in my Mom that made her incapable of protecting herself and her child from my Dad. And with understanding this illness, I can lay down my rage at her. I forgive her because I see her as a victim, as well. She is a victim of her father's abuse. She is a victim of the time period she lived in. She is a victim of society's ills. She is a victim of my father's abuse. When you view someone as mentally ill, it's much harder to be angry at them. I forgive her because she was doing the best she could given her mental illness. I understand how a sexually-abused woman with no counseling and no earning potential could behave the way she did. I forgive her.

I find it much harder to feel this level of forgiveness and understanding with my father. I don't know as much about him. He didn't talk about his childhood and I wasn't around his sisters as much to hear about the family stories or watch the relationship interactions. I know that his family was very poor as well. His family grew up in the houses provided by the mining companies and he would often steal coal from the trains that ran behind their house for heat during the winter. He and his buddies would jump a train a few miles down the track from their home. They would climb on top of the coal heaps on the open train cars and push the coal over the sides and down to the ground. They would continue this process until the train was a few miles on the other side of their homes. The boys would then jump off the train and begin gathering the coal and taking it home. In the winter, if they ran out of coal, he would have to jump a train and break away the ice and snow from the heaps of coal before he could start pushing the chunks of coal over the side of the train cars. I have a spike from that very same railway that ran behind my grandmother's home to remind me of my roots and the hardy stock of people I come from.

His family was poor and uncultured. Dad had six sisters and some of them were very warm and fun. Others were odd and stand-offish. My grandmother was a widow with children when she met Mr. Grimes. She was not in love with him but married him out of necessity. He died when I was three or four years old, so I don't remember what personality he had or how he treated my father. My Dad never told stories about him, either good or bad. That must mean something. It's like there were absolutely no emotional ties between my father and his father. He never, ever spoke of him.

My Grandma Grimes was a cranky, judgmental woman. I don't remember ever feeling a sense of love and warmth from her. Her hugs were stiff and cold, so maybe she treated my dad the same way growing up. But being poor and without a gentle mother doesn't make you a sexual pervert. I still wonder what happened to him that made him an abuser. Research says that most abusers were abused themselves. That's why sexual abuse is often generational and familial. I will probably never know the truth of his upbringing, but I believe there was some type of sexual abuse in his childhood that caused him to be a perpetrator. Sexual abuse of any kind is about having a feeling of power over another. It's not about the sex. Something happened in his childhood that left him feeling powerless and weak, and the sexual dominance made him feel powerful and strong. Like my mother, he suffered from a mental illness that caused him to act in horrendous ways. His sexual abuse of his daughter, and probably his wife, made him feel dominant and in-control. It helped hide his feelings of inadequacy and fear. It doesn't make me like him, but it does help me, in some small way, to forgive him.

If you don't know much about your parents' childhood, or even if you do, you may find this layer of forgiveness hard to comprehend and assimilate into your process of healing. Forgiveness can happen quickly with a divine insight or through a spiritual stream of grace. It may happen slowly over time as you let go of the anger and allow the insights and understandings to seep into your sense of knowing. It's never about saying that since I know my mom was abused, that makes it okay for her to have allowed my dad to abuse me. I simply understand a little more of what was happening in her mind. I understand my parents' sickness a little more.

With this understanding and with this forgiveness, I now see that *the abuse wasn't about me.* I used to wonder as a child, "What's wrong with me that my Dad hates me so much he wants to hurt me? What's wrong with me that my own mother won't protect me? Aren't I worth protecting?" I felt there was something inherently missing or wrong about me that my own parents didn't love and care for me. But with some understanding of my parents, I now know there's nothing inherently wrong with me. They were sick and I was unlucky enough to be in their sphere of influence. This knowledge helped me shed some of the feelings of unworthiness. No one thing helps it all to go away, but each new insight sheds light on who I really am. The layers of the onion fall away to reveal the divine soul that I am.

During my counseling, I read the book by Dr. Susan Forward called *Toxic Parents*. She calls sexual abuse the "ultimate betrayal," but on page 165, she says that "incest victims are usually the healthiest members of their families. After all, the victim usually has the symptoms—self-blame, depression, destructive behaviors, sexual problems, suicide attempts, substance abuse—while the rest of the family often seems outwardly healthy. But despite this, it is usually the victim who ultimately has the clearest vision of the truth." She goes on to say that because of all the emotional pain and the burden of keeping the family secret, the victim is usually the first to seek help to reclaim their dignity and their power.

Forgiveness is not about letting your perpetrator off the hook or about discounting the pain that you are feeling. It's about moving beyond your experiences and reclaiming your life. It's about letting go of the painful part of your memories so that you can make room for new experiences. By letting go, you can enjoy your present moment experiences without the filmy sludge of your past coloring your view. The memories will always be there, but the suffering can stop. Forgiveness is one more step you can take towards a life with no inner turmoil. Forgive and enjoy a newfound life of peace.

The Third Level of Forgiveness

The third level of forgiveness may be a real stretch for some of you. It deals with the idea of our spirituality and the path we have chosen. Depending on your culture or upbringing, reincarnation may feel very foreign to your personal religious concepts. But those who are ready to hear the Truth will know within the knowledge of what I'm sharing here. I now know that we are eternal Spirits who come to the Earth plane many times to learn lessons and evolve our souls. I've grown into this belief and it feels "right" for me. Let me share my exploration and acceptance of this topic.

You can be sure the Baptists didn't teach me about reincarnation! You had one life and you had better decide if you were going to get saved and go to heaven, or continue to be a sinner and go to hell when you died. One chance to do it right or forever burn in hell! That's a wonderful scare tactic and it works sometimes on people.

I remember being young, around six years old, and sitting in the pew at church. Rev. Powers was up at the pulpit ranting and raving about getting saved from the fiery depths of hell. He was waving the Bible around and pacing back and forth, yelling about the pearly gates and how we needed to give our life to Jesus and trust in the Lord. He preached that we were all filled with original sin and that only the blood of Jesus would redeem our souls from eternal damnation and yadda, yadda, yadda. He sometimes would get so wound up that he would cough up this white stuff and you could see it in his mouth as he was yelling! He'd take out his handkerchief and wipe it off his tongue and keep right on going. Yuck! What was that? I used to think. I still don't know what happened to him during these times, but he was definitely impassioned with his sermon, possessed by something. But as I listened to him, there would be this small wise voice inside me. It would say, "This isn't right. They've got it all wrong!"

I didn't know what the right way was, but I knew these folks had it all mixed up. I mentioned it to my parents that this wasn't the right way. They were, of course, startled to hear their young child tell them that their religion was wrong. They went to great lengths to discredit me or taunt me, and eventually threaten me, when I persisted with my opinion. So, I learned to just listen and go along in order to keep the peace, knowing very well these people were crazy. This inner knowing that the concepts taught by the Baptist church were wrong stayed with me throughout my elementary and early teen years. I had no choice in whether I went to church or not, but I knew these folks were confused about God. I was smart and so often posed difficult questions to the Sunday School teachers. I'd read the Bible and hear the stories and ask these piercing questions about topics that confused me. I often was ignored in Sunday School class or given some feeble answer. The Sunday School teachers often would just read the same contradictory verses out loud again, with more volume, as if that alone would clear up my confusion. I think I exhausted them. I wanted them to think about what they were saying about God, and they refused to do it. There was much more to God and Spirit than what they understood.

Okay, let's get back to the topic of reincarnation. There was one particularly memorable experience I had as a child. Several of our family vacations were two-week camping trips out West. We would leave by car on Friday evening and Dad would drive all night and day. By Saturday afternoon we would be in Colorado or Wyoming amidst the beautiful Rocky Mountains. We stopped in many of the little western towns, explored their museums and visited the tourist stops. On one trip when I was about nine or ten years old, we stopped in a little gold mining town and visited one of the museums along the wooden boardwalk of Main Street. As we walked in the front door of the renovated old home I felt an undeniable feeling of being there before. I mentioned it to my Dad. "I've been here before" I said to him, "I know this place." No he assured me. We've never been to this town, so I must be confusing it with one of the other places we had visited on another trip.

As we moved on into the house, the tour guide began explaining the history of the place. I tugged on my Dad's shirt again and said "I know this building!" and went on to describe the layout of the rooms on the first and second floors. As we walked through the building, the rooms were laid out exactly as I had described them. "See, I told you I've been here before! I know this place." Well, my parents looked at me and then each other as I described the setting of each room.

We proceeded upstairs and my folks looked on in horror as they meandered through the rooms on the second story. There were mannequins of men and women in each room dressed in period pieces from the Old Wild West. The women were scantily dressed. Some had their skirts hiked up to show off the little derringers tucked in their garters! Unbeknownst to them, my parents had taken us on a tour of a western bordello! And here was their young daughter describing the place! We were quickly hustled out of the museum and all questions were quieted with promises of ice cream and trinkets.

The strong sense of déjà vu that I had there was the most intense I have ever felt. How did I know the layout of that building? I didn't think too much about the incident from my childhood until I started reading about reincarnation and its effect on our present life. In a regression, I have "recalled" one lifetime in the Old West, where I was a single woman with a daughter running a small fabric store. A stranger comes into town who recognizes me as a former call girl at a bordello and I am worried that he will expose me and my cover story of being a widow to the townspeople. I find it interesting that I had been a call girl in a former life where I was abused and used by men and then I repeat that scenario again in this lifetime of being abused and used by a man.

As a teenager and young adult, I had heard about reincarnation and brought it up as a topic of discussion with people. My Dad and my church teachers handled it as simply a laughable topic. "Oh," someone would say, "It's where you come back again and again, like in India, and maybe you'll eventually come back as a cow!" So the idea of reincarnation was first presented as a crazy myth that uneducated people believed. Or it was a way of thinking that the powerful people in India used to keep the others in control. You were born into a certain level of the caste system and you stayed there your entire life. There was no chance of moving up the ladder of success or opportunity. The rich stayed rich and the poor stayed poor. So I shrugged off the idea of reincarnation as just another structured religious system that kept the ignorant masses in place. It played along with the only Karl Marx quote I knew that "religion was an opiate for the masses."

In college, I was exposed to more world cultures and historical stories. I read with interest how other people thought of God and how they worshipped this deity or panel of deities. None really felt right to me, at least not the dry account I got from a history text. I don't remember a course being offered in World Religions like they offer at colleges and universities today. Such classes are wonderful for broadening the world view of young minds who have had a very limited perspective on global issues. So, on my search for some spiritual exploration, college didn't help me much.

I did have a great sociology class with Professor Harkness at Kent State University, Stark Campus. I really enjoyed and respected his teachings and his approach to education. His lecture one day was about the importance of our family of origin on our psychosocial development. We discussed how the cultural and economic surroundings of our birth family influenced our world view, our expectations of life, and our sense of self. The roles that were played out in front of us were often thought to be the only ones that existed. Everybody around us lived pretty much this lifestyle, or very close to what we were seeing in our own family, so we most often felt that our lives would play out in a similar fashion. Our self esteem was formed at an early age, before school age, and would influence nearly every choice we made in our entire life, from career paths, to marriage, to hobbies, to raising a family, to simply how to be happy. And as that particular class was ending and we were gathering our books, Professor Harkness shouted out, "So the moral of the story is…choose your parents wisely!"

I was caught off guard by his comic comment and laughed out loud with the other students. *Yeah, right, as if we have a choice,* was my thought as I left the classroom. That was over 34 years ago. And yet I remember that one line vividly. Somewhere that comment about being able to choose our family of origin stuck in my consciousness and danced in my head. Little did I know that he was right! Years later, I would learn about how our spirits choose each lifetime, select the situation we are born into, decide what our parents are to be like, pick our gender and sexual orientation, opt for the hardships we would endure and the goals or lessons we wanted to attain. Read more about our pre-birth planning from Robert Schwartz's interesting book, *Your Soul's Plan: Discovering the Real Meaning of the Life You Planned Before You Were Born.* Michael Newton, Ph.D. also wrote about pre-birth planning in his wonderful books, *Journey of Souls* and *Destiny of Souls.*

At some point in my twenties, I heard about the actress Shirley MacLaine and her viewpoints about God and life and reincarnation. I had heard about her book, *Out on a Limb,* but felt somehow scared to read it. I remember mentioning it to my folks and they laughed it off as that ole kook, Shirley MacLaine! She's just an actress, so what would she know about religion? But, it was if I knew that reading that book would change me, and I wasn't really sure if I knew if that change would be for the better or not. I ignored the book for a couple of years, but eventually, after hearing about the book or seeing it several times over a few years, I finally was brave enough to buy the book and read it.

How can you be scared to read a book? The ego really doesn't want you to grow and change. It would rather latch onto old beliefs or continue feeling lost rather than know the truth. So Shirley told her story of how her current love was someone from a past life and how the two lifetimes were intertwined. I remember thinking it was interesting reading, but didn't put much credence into it. I tossed it aside as one more theory on my quest for spiritual information. But somewhere deep inside it planted a seed that would slowly grow. And I do mean slowly. Her book wasn't published until 1983. I probably read it in 1985 or 1986, and didn't really think much about reincarnation until years later.

Throughout my thirties, I continued on my spiritual quest, trying out various churches in the area and finding none that felt right. My massage therapist was an intelligent woman who knew more than me about alternative ways of thinking. As she worked the kinks out of my shoulders and back we would talk about all kinds of interesting topics. We had talked occasionally about past lives and she mentioned that she knew a local woman who performed past life regressions for people using hypnosis. My interest grew and I tried it out. Not as a true spiritual quest, you see, but more as an enjoyable Saturday afternoon pastime. I made the appointment with the hypnotist. She explained how the procedure went, gave me some subliminal messages and asked me to start breathing deeply. I went under very quickly. It took me a few minutes to get any images but slowly I found myself sitting in a large room filled with many books. It looked like a library in an older established home. I was a young girl sitting on the floor playing with my dog, an English Springer Spaniel. (I don't know dog breeds, so I had to look up a picture of the brown and white speckled, long-eared dog I was petting.) Behind me sat my father in a comfortable, over-sized leather chair. He was reading a newspaper and smoking a pipe. I remember feeling so peaceful there. Everything was safe there. It was comforting being in the library with all those books, and playing with my dog, and smelling the smoke of my father's pipe. I could look outside through some French doors onto our estate. The gardens were beautifully manicured with lots of places for me to play with my dog. There were even secret garden places where I could hide out by myself and play make-believe. The hypnotist asked me how old I was and I responded, "Eight." What country are you in? It's England. Was there anyone else in the room? No. Does your mother live there with you? Oh yes, but she's not in the room right now. Do you have servants? Yes, there is a housekeeper. She's lovely. The hypnotist then guided me to leave that lifetime and search for another. Together we explored a couple more lifetimes with her asking me simple, straightforward questions.

The hypnotist pulled me back into awareness. I opened my eyes and started laughing. I couldn't believe what I had just seen. Was all that for real? Or was my imagination just running wild on me and making up these scenarios? The hypnotist didn't guide me through the important questions about each lifetime. I now know that a trained regression hypnotist will ask many types of critical questions of the person going through the regression so as to pull some value from the session. My hypnotist didn't ask what lesson was to be learned from that life, what the significance was for the scenes that I recalled, how I died in each lifetime, or what issues in that lifetime may have rolled over to my current life. She didn't allow me to experience the process of death. That one incident alone can really change people's attitude about death and dying. You can really feel the whole experience of being a spirit that continues on, a spirit that has eternal life.

So, I left there thinking, "That was fun!" It was surely entertaining, but the experience really didn't help me put much credibility in the process of past-life regression or the concept of reincarnation. I didn't come away with a real appreciation of how hypnosis and regression can assist therapists in dealing with current issues in their clients. It didn't shed any light on anything I was dealing with in my current lifetime. It also didn't help strengthen my spiritual beliefs or open any doors on my quest for understanding. I left thinking that regression was simply a parlor game.

But since that time, I have had other past-life and between-life regressions by more qualified hypnotists. I have learned about lifetimes where I was a male living in England, supporting my family making shoes and other items from leather. I was once a priest or wise elder in ancient Japan, naming the town I lived in and describing the kinds of trees that grow there. I was able to Google the town's name and found there was a city by that name in southern Japan and then found the exact trees that are native to that area. I had never heard of this city or the trees before my regression.

I have read many accounts about regressions and their influence on the here and now. Many books have been written about reincarnation, past-life regressions, and pre-birth planning that help us understand this process of choosing to be born again and again for the evolution of our souls. Sylvia Browne talks of accounts of reincarnation and pre-birth planning in her numerous books. Psychologist Dr. Edith Fiore wrote *You Have Been Here Before* recounting how her patients have gone into previous existences to find the sources of their talents, strengths and problems and made remarkable recoveries from long standing issues. *Your Soul's Plan,* Discovering the Real Meaning of the Life You Planned Before You Were Born, written by Robert Schwartz, recounts the stories of ten individuals who visit their pre-birth planning sessions, learn why each decided to experience challenges in their life, and understand how they as a soul created their life blueprint.

Here is what I understand right now. I do believe that our spirits return to the earthly plane for as many times as they want. My spirit, this time, chose to be born into a dysfunctional family where the father was abusive to me mentally, emotionally, physically and sexually. I chose to have a mother who was weak, dependent on my father for everything and totally incapable of protecting me. During a between-life regression, I stood in a grand hall with my soul group seated around me. My spirit guides, along with masters from the other side, were there to add their guiding words. I asked members of my soul group to play the roles of my father and mother, siblings and other important players in my life. All agreed except for the two souls I asked to be my parents. They did not want to take on such hideous roles and hurt me during my coming existence. I begged them to do this for me—to lower their frequency so much that they could assume these personalities. They eventually, reluctantly, agreed. I needed someone to play those parts, so that I could be in the position of being abused and abandoned.

I chose to come to Earth this time to see if I could learn the lesson of forgiveness. It is the hardest of all lessons to learn in this illusion we call our life. Our ego loves to hold on to grudges and injustices. It gains strength from the anger and resentment we feel. We hang on to the idea of revenge. We think that retaliation is justified in order to right the wrongs that have been done to us. The ego urges us to continue to be angry and judgmental. The ego tells us we have a right to be mad!

Or maybe instead of anger, we continue to play the victim role. We allow others to treat us unsatisfactorily. We have poor boundaries and stay in relationships that are not good for us. Instead of releasing the pain, and start really living our lives, we wallow in the misery and despair of hopelessness and pain. We see the world through gray-colored glasses and assume bad luck will come our way. We feel shame for living the way we do and unworthy of reaching for more. When we daydream we don't see the possibilities of the future, but rather see our relationships failing, money being scarce and goals fading farther away. Everything is gloomy and unpromising. Our ego loves this state of mind too. When we're vibrating at the lowest levels, the ego is in control.

Dr. David Hawkins shows us in his Map of Consciousness that when you are experiencing the feelings of shame, guilt, and apathy, you are vibrating at the lowest of the emotional levels. Grief and fear are slightly above them, but all of these low levels of consciousness are controlled by the ego. It uses fear and all the related emotional baggage to keep us functioning at our lowest possible level of unconsciousness. If we raise our vibration to the higher level of anger, we are moving forward but the ego is still in control and keeps us bound to the past.

I bounced between these various states of mind. I held onto the anger, but showed it in passive-aggressive ways. My sarcasm and critical nature picked at those I came in contact with and especially those I was most intimately involved with. I would dive into depressions from the shame and guilt and come out with a low-grade form of apathy towards everything, all the while pretending to be perfectly happy with my life.

If we can see that we chose this life and all of the situations that come before us, then we can step back as the observer and look at the situation from a more distant point of view. We can be more objective in seeing the situation and react in more loving ways. We can choose to forgive. And when we do, we lift beyond the material reality and step into a world full of spirit and loveliness.

My third level of forgiveness came with the realization that the spirits who are now playing the roles of my Mother and Father are spirits within my soul group who agreed to take on these roles so that I could take on my own challenge. I chose to take on this lifetime filled with childhood sexual abuse. I planned it out, just as I would plan out an itinerary for a vacation. I asked my kindred souls to play the parts of my abusive father and my weak mother and they reluctantly agreed. I chose to take on this responsibility to see if I could wake up to who I really am, a divine, sacred, eternal Spirit. I planned that if I did wake up enough, I would write a book about these spiritual recovery methods and help other individuals heal. I came here in this incarnation to remember who I really am, and to help others claim their divinity and heal from their abuse. On an even larger scale, I came here this time to help heal the Earth, to help balance the masculine and feminine energies that exist here. As I write this, it feels like a tremendous burden, but yet I somehow know that it is true.

As your consciousness or spirituality grows, try being the observer of your life. Step back and look at your life as if it is a movie or play and watch the characters interact. Every person and every conflict is a lesson that either you planned and the other person agreed to help you learn, or they planned the lesson and you agreed to help them learn. That's what all of life is about. Can you navigate through the trials and tribulations of life and still come from a place of love? Can you raise your level of consciousness so that you feel the oneness of all that exists no matter what the circumstances?

When we have attained a level of higher consciousness, we will be able to see that even the person who terribly abused us has a Sacred Heart, just like us. When we can see that our abuser is a scared and lonely soul who feels so totally less than everyone else, who feels that he/she is nowhere close to God and feels hopeless and unloved and worthless, can we see how their behavior is just a by-product of the vast distance between them and God, a symptom of the self-loathing and inadequacy they feel. And when this big step happens, this realization that even our abuser is a child of God, we can inch closer to the huge of step of forgiveness. When you have compassion for your abuser, you have truly stepped into your own Sacred Heart. You have become the Light.

Part VI:
Summary

Summary

This book has been a journal of my recovery journey that I have chosen to share with you. The process of writing these pages has led me to fuller self awareness and hopefully will help you to heal from the traumatic sexual abuse you experienced. The specific details of our sexual abuse stories will be unique to each of us, but the ensuing problems in our lives have common elements. We may suffer from low self-worth, have problems with relationships and experience various levels of depression, sometimes lasting for years. We may endure bouts of anxiety and feelings of not being good enough, or may spend our lives trying to get everyone to like us. Even with the best counseling, there may be an underlying heaviness or emptiness to our existence. We are vibrational beings and the sexual abuse has knocked our frequency askew. We must regain our natural frequency before we can truly become 'in sync' with ourselves.

That's where Spirituality steps in and helps us fully recover. By becoming aware of our Sacred Heart and filling it with the Light of Spirit, we can overcome any abuse that was ever been done to us. Divine Love will help curb the cravings, light the darkness and soothe the jagged edges. Spirituality raises our vibration from feelings of fear, shame and anger to love, serenity and transcendence. It may be difficult at first to acknowledge that you are a Sacred Being of Light, but through the methods I've described in this book, you can claim your divinity and experience the Pearl of Peace. Your natural frequency can be restored to its fullest potential so that you can live a peace-filled, happy life.

If there is only one element that you put into practice from this book I hope it will be the start of a meditation practice. Meditation will help you find the Center Point of Peace that dwells within your body between your heart and belly button. Only by quieting the mind and going into the stillness, will you experience the peace that is your birthright. The Pearl of Peace exists within you, but you must get quiet to find this beautiful place. And in landing here, you'll start healing from the inside out.

As you meditate, invite your spirit guides and guardian angels to make themselves known to you. Inquire about their names. Ask for their guidance and assistance with issues in your life. Feel their presence. Feel their vibration. Merge with the vibration of your higher self to gain the wisdom that is inherently yours. It doesn't matter what type of meditation you do or what religion you are. Sit down, get quiet, and nurture your spiritual essence.

Each time you sit down in meditation, your inner spirit grows stronger. Your Divine Light burns a little brighter. Your vibration rises. As this essence grows, your Sacred Heart continues to fill with Love and Light. As your essence grows inside the Sacred Heart, it slowly pushes the dents in the Sacred Heart outward making you feel more normal and less damaged. Your feeling of being less than others diminishes as you own your true power, the power of the Sacred Heart. Feelings of anxiety and depression fade away as you start feeling more connected to your body and to the universe. You know you are a part of something much larger than you—something mystical and wonderful. The "fight or flight" mechanism is able to gently slow down as your emotional body calms down. The endless negative chatter of the 'monkey mind' relaxes into serene tranquility. Your mind, body and spirit all benefit from sitting quietly in the silence.

Add other nurturing practices to your daily life for faster and deeper recovery. Become aware of your incessant internal dialogue and replace negative thoughts with more uplifting affirmations. Surround yourself with beautiful, healing music. Join a drum circle, or if there's none available in your area, start one! Enjoy the beautiful call-and-response chanting of a Kirtan in your community. Find someone who specializes in singing bowls and tuning forks and take part in their services. Replace the newspaper and evening news with inspirational messages in the many wonderful books I've mentioned. Only bring higher vibrational people and activities into your life.

To help your physical body heal, try getting a monthly massage to work out the tension buried in the cells of your tissues. Join a yoga class to feel the benefits of an ancient practice. Spend time in nature. Dance.

Find a spiritual group of people who uplift your being with their very presence. Even though I do not attend a Unity Church at this time, I would highly recommend finding a Unity Church or other New Thought organization in your area. It is so important to have like-minded people around while recovering from our past traumas. The compassion and peacefulness of these spirit-filled individuals will add another wonderful dimension to your life.

Let's review and remember the deeper meanings of the five Unity principles and how we can apply them to our lives. Here are the five principles written again as personal affirmations:

1. God is absolute good. God is present with me everywhere I go.
2. I have a Spark of Divinity within me. My very essence is of God and, therefore, I am inherently good and worthwhile.
3. I create my experiences with the activity of my mind. Everything has its start in my thoughts.
4. My prayers are creative thinking that heightens the connection with the Divine. They therefore bring forth wisdom, healing, prosperity, and everything good.

5. I know and understand the Laws of Life, that everything is connected through frequencies. But knowing this Truth is not enough. I must live the truth I know and consciously raise my vibration from shame, fear and anger to love.

Forgiveness may be one of the more difficult areas to accomplish on your healing journey. The forgiveness process may come in various levels and phases, with your anger and bitter feelings subsiding for awhile, and then reemerging as new information surfaces to your awareness. Be gentle with yourself as you learn to let go of the emotional entanglements with your abuser and, possibly, the non-abusing parent. Remember that harboring feelings of anger and resentment only affect you—your body, your peace of mind, your emotional state. Your abuser does not suffer any damage from your low-grade fury and irritable moods. Forgiveness does not condone the abuser's behavior. It simply lets you drop the ugly sack of rage and move on to a peaceful life. Ask your angels for assistance with this area. This is a biggie! Don't feel like you have to do it alone. Ask your higher self to help you forgive what happened to you and to help you stop playing the victim role in your life.

You are not alone on your journey to wellness. Pray to God and all his/her divine spiritual helpers for assistance in getting your life in order. I was able to use the spiritual practices mentioned in this book to help me fully heal from the sexual abuse from my father. May you find the Pearl of Peace that resides within you and live a heart-centered life. I send love from my Sacred Heart to yours.

Part VII:
Afterword

My Father's Death

Afterword: My Father's Death

My father died during the final editing process of this book. He was 89 years old. He experienced heart failure while driving on a major highway and passed out with my mom in the passenger seat. She was able to maneuver the car out of the median strip, hitting a guard rail, but came to rest safely on the side of the road. Dad died in the car, but was resuscitated by paramedics and taken to a local hospital. He was put in a drug-induced coma for 30 hours to help with his recovery process. He regained consciousness at times and was even able to get off the ventilator, but his condition worsened and he made his transition eleven days later.

I hadn't been near him in years and I didn't know if I wanted to see him again. It felt very confusing. What was I supposed to do? A daughter *should* go see her dying father, but this was quite different. Did I even want to see him again? But through the confusion came a clear understanding of what I needed to do. I went to the hospital while he was in the drug-induced coma. He looked so frail and small, not the huge man I was so afraid of. I thanked him for playing the part I had asked of him and told him he would now understand the whole picture of what had transpired. I told him all was forgiven and that he should go to the Light. I assured him that he was not going to hell, that there was no hell, and that his loved ones would be waiting for him. I urged him several times to go to the Light.

I visited him again on the day he died. He was in hospice and heavily drugged for the pain. My brothers were in the room with me this time and I cringed as they held his hands. Those hands had been on me too many times. I never wanted them to touch me again. We stayed for just a while, but as we left I again told him to go to the Light. I didn't want him to be afraid that he was going to hell for what he had done and become an earthbound spirit. He needed to know it was safe to go to the Light.

He died later that evening and after I got the phone call I felt numb. It felt surreal. He was gone. He could no longer hurt me. But then the flood of emotions took over. They would enter and leave in such rapid succession that I couldn't even explain them fast enough. It was such a roller-coaster ride of feelings for the next week or so. It felt like I was going crazy.

Maybe it will help you if I list some of the feelings and thoughts I experienced during the days after his death. These are in no specific order, but I would jump from one to the other and then to another and then back to an earlier one and then to another one and then… you get the picture. I don't know if folks who have not been abused have this kind of jumbled thought process and chaotic feelings, but here's some of what I experienced:

- I felt a deep sadness come over me, like a strong wave of energy hitting my body. I didn't understand this sadness, because I had really grieved the loss of my parents 25 years ago when the memories surfaced. So I asked my inner self what I was feeling sad about and I became seven years old again and looking at my Daddy's face. He's smiling at me and I feel such joy for being with him. This little girl just realized she'd lost her Daddy.
- I felt a sense of revenge! "Good!" I heard myself say inside. "Now I can start living my life!" This line certainly surprised

me. I'm 58 years old and thought I had been really living my life. Obviously, a part of me has not.
- I felt relief. Now I can publish my book without fear of him killing me.
- I felt a sense of freedom. Now I don't have to worry about running into him at a store or restaurant. Maybe now I can go to a family reunion.
- I'm feeling sad again. But now I'm feeling guilty. What would my friends say to me? They're all angry at him in defense of me. Shouldn't I be angry at him too? If I tell my friends I'm sad, they'll think I'm crazy. They'll say "What??!! How can you be sad when he did those things to you?" Now I'm feeling ashamed that I'm sad. Oh sheesh!
- I'm feeling so angry at him right now! He took the secret to the grave. He could have told someone the truth before he died.
- I'm feeling compassion for his soul. He now understands the part he was playing in my journey.
- I'm feeling sad again. Sad for my whole life. There was so much fear and trauma and sadness during my entire life. In my entire family. So much dysfunction. He played his part well. Almost too well.
- I'm afraid of going to the funeral. My mom doesn't want me there. Will the family members shun me, call me names, point at me?
- I feel so much anger at not being heard …again! Of not being believed…again!
- I'm now looking at this situation from my higher self again, being the observer. Watching it all play out from a higher vantage point. It gives me much greater perspective. I have peace.
- I feel relief. I actually had to see him dead to feel safe.
- I felt anger during the funeral service as folks said all these

- "saintly" things about my dad. They don't want to know the whole picture about him.
- At the funeral, my cousin's wife spoke about how "safe" the women in the family felt when Dad was around. Isn't that an odd speech to give as a eulogy? I'm thinking the women may have felt safe around him, but the children surely didn't.
- I feel such confusion in my head. The rapid succession of thoughts and emotions leaves me feeling dizzy.
- I feel like I'm going crazy! I feel the emotions on the physical plane and then change to seeing things from a higher perspective, from a spiritual plane. There was this sense of being in my body and then not being in my body and very quickly traveling back and forth. I would be sensing through my eyes and ears and then sensing from about two feet above my head.

EXAMPLES:

- I'm feeling some sort of revenge and anger towards my parents, and then instantly flip to realizing my Dad now understands the part I asked him to play. He sees the whole picture now. Then I'd flip back to feeling sadness for the deep grief my brothers were experiencing.
- I'm feeling anger at the funeral because I haven't been invited to tell my view of Dad, and then changing to this ethereal place where I hear myself saying in my head, "Forgive them, Father, for they know not what they do." This sure surprised me, because I'm not a devout Christian. Why am I repeating Jesus' words?
- I'm feeling angry with my Mom. She doesn't want me at the funeral. She says I've caused so many problems in our family. I didn't do anything wrong! It was done to me!
- I feel sad as I remember all the good parts of Dad. He was a hard worker and a good provider for his family. He was

honest and good at fixing anything mechanical. He taught me how to water ski, drive a boat, and how to catch a fish. He took me on countless camping trips and wonderful, long vacations. I've been in just about every state in the country because of him.

- I feel so sad because he never told me he loved me.
- I feel so sad because he never told me he was proud of me.
- I feel angry because of the way he divided our family against each other. He would pit one or more of us against another. He'd have us make fun of Mom or Mark, in a very mean way.
- I feel confused. What do I say to people when they ask how I'm doing? What I'm feeling?
- I feel spacey. Sometimes I feel distant, not connected or grounded, numb. Then I feel transcendent, like an observer. Looking at things from my higher self. I definitely feel spacey.
- I feel anger. Why do I have to be the outsider in the family? I was the victim, not the abuser! Why are they honoring him?
- I feel proud. I may have stood in the foyer of the funeral home greeting friends and family as they came to the calling hours, rather than in the main room with my family, but I was there. I'm showing my face to the world that I'm still here.
- I feel gratitude for my dear husband. He holds me when I need to cry, he listens when I need to talk and he takes my hand and says, "Let's go" when I needed to go to the hospital or funeral home, without ever questioning why.

This is just a small sampling of the emotional turmoil I experienced during this time. I was amazed at how quickly I would jump from one emotion to another in rapid succession. The racing thoughts and sensual experiences definitely made me feel that I was not in control. It was that inner voice that never shuts up on a major dose of adrenaline. Just be with your feelings and don't react to any of them. Let them pass. They will pass.

THE FUNERAL

I had decided to attend the funeral even though my mother didn't want me there. Some of my friends were even surprised that I wanted to go, but I felt it was necessary on many levels for me to be there. I'm not saying everyone should do this, but for me, it was what I needed to do. First of all, I needed to see him dead. I needed to see the physical evidence that he was no longer a threat to me.

I needed the extended family to see that I wasn't some sort of crazy person. I'm not sure what my parents have told the family about me over the years, but I needed them to see that I'm a normal, productive member of society.

I had a right to be there. Even though he did terrible things to me, he was still my Dad and I needed to be part of this ritual. My mom didn't want me to attend, but that made me determined to be there. I deserved to be there and she wasn't going to stop me from being a part of this family gathering.

And for some reason, I needed to show that I was strong! I needed to show myself, my Mom and my family that I wasn't afraid of facing them.

But I was afraid. The morning of his funeral, I was feeling very scared and doubting my decision to go. I didn't want to cause a scene with my Mom at the funeral home, but I didn't know what her reaction would be when I showed up. I didn't know how my extended family, my numerous aunts, uncles and cousins would treat me. Would I be shunned and left standing alone and isolated.

I was crying softly in my cup of tea when I picked up a little book a friend had given me months before. She and I are co-facilitators in a healing group for survivors of sexual abuse and she had suggested that we use it in our healing circle. I had been remiss in not reading it. It was called *You Are Special* by Max Lucado. It's a tiny book written for children about a group of wooden people named the Wemmicks. They were all made by a wood carver and all day, every day, they would put stickers on each other. Some were golden stars and the others were gray dots. The pretty, talented, athletic people would get lots of golden stars, while the older, chipped, untalented people would get lots of dots. Obviously, the stickers affected their egos and made them feel either okay or not-okay about themselves.

But one Wemmick had no stickers. The stickers didn't stick to this one little girl. A sad and hurting little Wemmick boy asked her why the stickers didn't stick to her. She talked with him and urged him to visit the woodcarver to find out why the stickers didn't stick to her. And so he did. The woodcarver explained to the wooden boy that he, the wood carver, didn't care what the other Wemmicks thought about the boy. The woodcarver made the boy and thought he was very special. The woodcarver explained that what the Wemmicks think about you doesn't matter. All that matters is what I think of you and I think you're very special. The stickers only stick if they matter to you. The more you trust my love, the less you care about the stickers and eventually, the stickers won't stick anymore.

Through divine timing, this beautiful, little story became my lifeline that day. It lifted me out of my insecurity and gave me the strength to be me—a beautiful creation of God. It didn't matter what my Mom or relatives might say to me at the funeral. None of it would stick. I read the story to Wayne and "The dots don't stick" became our mantra for the day. Wayne and I said it out loud and giggled as we got out of the car and entered the funeral home. My mother and I stayed a healthy distance away from each other, and the other family members were thrilled to see me. My brothers wanted me there and were glad I had come. I thank Spirit for helping me with this beautiful little children's story that day.

MANY GIFTS

There were many gifts that came from my Dad's passing. I don't know that any are more important than the other but I'll share the several gifts I received from his transition to the spirit world.

My two brothers were real troupers through this whole thing. They took care of Mom and handled the details of Dad's care and funeral, while juggling the tenuous situation of keeping me informed of his declining health and eventual death, and keeping the peace with Mom. I hadn't been around my parents for 25 years, so my brothers didn't know how involved or informed I wanted to be. They simply asked, "Do you want to know what's going on? Do you want to come to the hospital for a visit? Do you want to be at the funeral?" Mark especially was so genuine right after Dad's heart attack in stating that he didn't know how to handle the situation between me and my parents. I so appreciated his honesty and candor and assured him that his confusion was normal. He was afraid I would be angry at him for decisions he made or for not keeping me informed on a timely basis. I assured him that there's no Emily Post guidance on funeral etiquette for a victim and her perpetrator. I simply asked him to keep me informed of Dad's prognosis. A few days later, my youngest brother would fly in from Louisiana, and they both managed the situation with grace and gentleness.

A true gift from this experience was the increased feeling of closeness and intimacy that came between me and my brothers. The genuine conversations that occurred over dinner, in the hospital, at the funeral and at my home created a bond that feels so strong. Dad divided our family with his actions and words, but his death united us into a wonderful trio that I don't quite have words for. The connections we three siblings made during that tumultuous two week period have united us in genuine friendship. My husband commented to all of us on how amazingly deep our conversations were and how we handled such difficult times with grace and humor. I was even able to share with my brothers that I occasionally get messages from the spirit world. I asked them if they believed that our loved ones who have passed greet us on the other side when we die. They both believed this happens, so I explained that I had received two messages from the other side from my aunt and grandmother, my Dad's sister and mother-in-law. I asked my brothers to tell Dad that Skinny and Rhodie, their beloved nicknames, were waiting for him with open arms.

It is truly amazing that of all three of us handled my father's death with no fighting, no ill words and no hurt feelings with all the tension that existed around his passing. The deep respect and strong relationship my brothers and I have with each other now is truly a gift.

The picture below was taken in my home the day after my father's funeral. We were looking at old photo albums and remembering the fun times we had as kids. Notice the orb above my head. I believe that is my father's spirit joining us in the memories.

Mark, Jeanne and John—Day after the funeral.

The timing of my Dad's passing was also a gift. As I neared the completion of my book, I spoke often to Wayne and my friends of my fear of Dad's retaliation. He always told me he would kill me if I told anyone of the abuse, and here I was announcing it to the world in a very public way. It was very easy for me to visualize him learning about the book and then coming to my house or workplace and shooting me and then himself. A murder-suicide would have been his cowardly way out.

But instead he chose to leave this world. He removed this threat of danger for me by taking himself out of the physical plane. He certainly did not decide this on a physical level, but his higher self knew that I was afraid to go forward with publishing my book and speaking about my experiences. His timing was impeccable and has created a calming sense of relief for me. He checked out at a perfect time.

Last week after lunch, I was getting out of my car and walking back into the office, when I saw a car in the parking lot with a man inside who looked similar to him. I knew that he drove past my home and workplace on occasion, so when I saw this man I felt alarmed and drew in a quick breath. But then I assured myself that "No, he's dead now." I'm sure it will take some time for it to really sink in that he's gone and that I'm finally safe, but now I know the intimidation and danger that I feared are gone. He can't hurt me anymore. I'm now safe to go forward with what I was born to do and that is truly a gift.

As I've said before, I've never been one to ask for help. I've still got this independent streak that says I have to go it alone, always be strong and never show weakness. But this time I allowed myself to ask for help. When I heard about my father's heart attack, I started texting my friends about what was happening. I asked for their prayers and healing energy. I asked them to pray for my Dad and my family, that he would pass smoothly and that the family would experience little chaos and pain. I told them I was confused about what I was feeling and that I needed their support. I kept them abreast of the situation with regular updates from my phone. I had never done this before. I had never asked for help in such a public way and, I must say, the results were astounding. When I was feeling overwhelmed with emotion, I could feel this palpable cushion of love surround me and the emotion would ease. It felt like being hugged by a huge glazed donut. I would feel calm inside instead of the intense anger or grief that seemed to want to burst me open from the inside out. A simple phrase or word of encouragement would be just what I needed at the time. Sometimes a saying would get me through a tense situation. One friend texted me and said "You have the tools you need to handle this." She was so right! I did have the spiritual, intellectual, emotional and psychological tools to get me through this. She believed in me and reminded me of my strengths. I would repeat that phrase in my head when I was feeling weak or scared.

At times, I felt like I was holding onto one of my girlfriends' hands. It was like someone was literally walking with me through a particular emotion or situation. The power of my friends' energy and love was so immense that I stand in awe of it. I had prayed and sent healing energy to many people over the years, but I had never allowed myself to be on the receiving end of it. Why had I deprived myself of this wonderful feeling of being loved for so long? I think my sense of self-worth had finally grown enough to know I was worthy of their love.

I loved the honesty of my friends. They felt confused, just like me, and would candidly say, "I don't know what to say to you." Was I feeling angry, relieved, sad? Was I grieving in a weird sort of way? They didn't know whether to join me in a cheer that he was finally dead or console me for my loss? Their confusion was as evident as mine. So, we were just honest with each other. We'd talk about our feelings and they'd let me share my good memories of him. They distracted me with walks and activities and would just "be" with me. Their presence was a wonderful gift, whether in person or from afar. My father's death allowed me to give myself a gift by allowing my friends inside my inner circle where they could share my confusion, my raw emotions, my fragileness. I allowed myself to lean on them for comfort and strength. I have grown because of this experience and that is a gift.

HIS VISITS

I've now had two spiritual visits from my father and it has only been three weeks since his death. The first was a dream-like occurrence where he and I were suspended in space about 50 yards apart. At first, I didn't know who it was but as we drifted towards each other I could see his smiling face and knew it was him. He appeared to be about 35 years old and very handsome. I felt alarmed to be near him, but we quickly embraced and the dream was over. The whole thing lasted for what seemed about 2 seconds and I awoke with a start. It was so quick that I wasn't sure if it was real or not. But my doubts were short-lived.

The next day I was cooking breakfast. I made Wayne his sausage and eggs and he sat down to eat. I was frying my two eggs, leaving one as a "dippy" egg so I could dip my toast in the yolk. As I broke the other yolk so it would fry up in the pan, I heard my father say, "Yea, that's the way I like it, too!"

I spun around and looked at Wayne and said, "My father's here." I told him what I had heard and we discussed how my dream from the day before must have been real. Hearing my father's voice confirmed that yesterday's dream was indeed a spiritual visit from my Dad. I continued frying my eggs and sat down to eat with my toast and juice. As I took my first bite, my father came to me again and said "You're doing good, girl! I'm really proud of you!" Well, I had just written the above paragraphs earlier in the morning about how he had never told me he was proud of me. It really hit a nerve and I started crying. I shared with Wayne this new communication from my Dad and I told him that I had just written about this very idea an hour before. Wayne comforted me and was actually excited to know that I was connecting with my Dad in a new way.

I calmed down and we started to eat again, when a new wave of my father's presence hit me. His presence was so strong that I could actually feel him around me and I was overcome with panic. My core reaction to him for years had been fear and this was no different. I became so scared. I started crying again so hard that Wayne came over and knelt down by my chair and held me as I let the feeling pass.

Wayne shared with me that this feeling of fear will diminish as I learn to have a new relationship with my Dad. Wayne had learned this through contact with his departed grandfather who had sexually abused him. He assured me that the first few visits from his grandfather's spirit felt threatening, but that quickly changed. Wayne now knows his grandfather's visits are of care and concern and they have a new relationship based on love and respect. Their communication is now soul-to-soul, rather than based on the personalities that existed on the Earthly plane.

I mentioned to Wayne that I was glad this experience didn't happen while I was driving or at work because it was so intense and unsettling, but Wayne assured me that my Dad had planned this first visit very carefully. Dad made sure that I was somewhere safe and not alone. Wayne shared that Dad knew this would be hard for me at first, so he made sure I was safe at home and with Wayne when he made his presence known to me.

This is all still very raw for me. I don't know how often, or if, my Dad will visit me again. I'm glad that he is now free of the shame and guilt that must have plagued him here while he was alive. He is now aware and understands the part he played in my lifetime—the role I asked him to play as my abuser. If I am truly able to develop a new and loving relationship with my Dad on the spiritual plane, it will be the ultimate gift from his passing.

The spiritual practices I've outlined in this book assisted me in coping with my father's death. Meditation helped calm the anxiety that surrounded his final days and the resulting funeral. It helped me find my center, my Pearl of Peace. I practiced self-nurturance through the use of music, journaling, and rest. I opened myself up by sharing the whole experience with friends and allowing them to be an intimate part of my pain. I leaned on them for comfort and support and they surrounded me with love and healing.

The whirlwind of inner chatter was truly amazing during this time. I used my practice of being the spectator and observing the chatter that raced through my head. I consciously worked on being detached from the thoughts and strived at not getting sucked into every emotion that swept through me. I asked Spirit for help. I constantly asked the angels and spirit guides to rally round me as I negotiated my feelings and my family. I practiced forgiveness for my Dad and my family. They were all doing the best they could. I practiced affirmations by saying "The dots don't stick" as I navigated the funeral that day. It helped me reframe the event and allowed me to feel confident and self-assured.

This final episode in my relationship with my father has allowed me to use all the tools I've developed through counseling and spirituality to not only survive a difficult time, but grow because of it. My sincere hope is that you too will find the tools you need in this book to live a peaceful, rewarding life, to not just survive your past but to thrive in each precious, present moment.

Love and Light,
Jeanne

About the Author

JEANNE GRIMES BROOKS is a survivor of childhood sexual abuse that lasted over twelve years. She used traditional counseling and metaphysical methods to heal her mind, body and spirit from the abuse. She earned her Bachelor of Science degree from Kent State University in Secondary Education with certifications in mathematics and social studies. She has a Master's degree in Educational Technology from the University of Akron. Jeanne currently works on the Training and Documentation team at a computer software firm. She lives on a lake in Ohio with her wonderful husband, Wayne, and their brilliant cat, Maggie.

Appendix
Music List

CD Name	Artist	Recording	Website
Healing Music			
Atlantis Angelis	Patrick (Bernhardt) Bernard	Shining Star Music	www.patrickbernard.com
Bach for the Bath	Produced by Michael Maxwell	Avalon Music	
Conferring with the Moon	William Ackerman	Windham Hill Records	www.windham.com
Day Without Rain, A	Enya	Warner Music	www.enya.com
Dream Manifestation	Ron Clearfield	Dunrite Productions	ww.ronclearfield.com
Healing Journey, The	Tami Briggs, Therapeutic Harpist	Musical Reflections, Inc.	www.musicalreflections.com

In Memory of Trees	Enya	Warner Music	www.enya.com
Mozart Effect, The	Compiled by Don Campbell	Atlantic Recording	www.mozarteffect.com
• Volume I – Strengthen The Mind	Compiled by Don Campbell	Atlantic Recording	www.mozarteffect.com
• Volume II – Heal the Body	Compiled by Don Campbell	Atlantic Recording	www.mozarteffect.com
• Volume III – Unlock the Creative Spirit	Compiled by Don Campbell	Atlantic Recording	www.mozarteffect.com
Music for Brainwave Massage	Dr. Jeffrey Thompson	The Relaxation Company	www.therelaxationcompany.com
New Beginning, A	Jacob "Laughing Fox" Fitch		
Prayer-A Multi-Cultural Journey of Spirit	Various Artists	Soundings of the Planet	www.soundings.com
Prayer for the Wild Things	Paul Winter	Living Music	www.livingmusic.com
Seasons of the Soul	Lisa Lynne	Windham Hill Records	www.windham.com
Star Nations	Douglas Blue Feather	Blue Feather Productions	www.douglasbluefeather.com
Time for Peace, A: Ivory Sessions	Maranatha Singers	Warner Music	www.maranathamusic.com
Voice From Within	Michael Searching Bear	Searching Bear Flutes	www.searchingbearflutes.com
White Stones	Secret Garden	Phillips	www.secretgarden.no

Winter Solstice III (Christmas)	Windham Hill Artists	Windham Hill	www.windham.com
Woman's Voice, A	Compilation of Faire Celts	Narada World	www.narada.com
Chanting Music			
Chant	The Benedictine Monks of Santo Domingo De Silos	ANGEL Records	
Heart As Wide As The World	Krishna Das	Blackwood Music	www.krishnadasmusic.com
Into the Bliss	David Newman	Inner Fire Music	www.davidnewmanmusic.com
Toning			
HU, A Love Song to God	Eckankar	Eckankar	www.eckankar.org/hu
In The OM Zone	Steven Halpern	Inner Peace Music	www.innerpeacemusic.com
Singing Bowls			
Crystal Rainbow – Healing Soundtrack	Jay Schwed	Crystal Vision	www.HealingCrystalBowls.com
Crystal Rainbow – Chakra Balancing	Jay Schwed	Crystal Vision	www.HealingCrystalBowls.com

BIBLIOGRAPHY

Bass, Ellen and Davis, Laura, *The Courage to Heal, A Guide for Women Survivors of Child Sexual Abuse*. New York: Harper and Row, 1988.

Benson, Herbert, M.D., *The Relaxation Response*. New York: Avon Books, 1975.

Campbell, Don, *The Mozart Effect, Tapping the Power of Music t Heal the Body, Strengthen the Mind, and Unlock the Creative Spirit*. New York: Avon Books, 1997.

Chopra, Deepak, M.D., *Perfect Health*. New York: Three Rivers Press, 1991.

Dyer, Wayne, *The Power of Intention, Learning to Co-create Your World Your Way*. Carlsbad, CA: Hay House, Inc., 2004.

Emoto, Masuru, M.D., *Miraculous Messages from Water, How Water Reflects our Consciousness*. Hillsboro, Oregon: Beyond Words Publishing, 2004.

Fiore, Edith, M.D., *You Have Been Here Before: A Psychologist Looks at Past Lives*. Merrimack, NH: National Guild of Hypnotists, Inc., 2005.

Forward, Susan, M.D., *Toxic Parents*. New York: Bantam Books, 1989.

Foundation for Inner Peace, *A Course in Miracles*. Temecula, CA: Foundation for Inner Peace, 1976.

Grossman, Warren, Ph.D., *To Be Healed by the Earth*. New York, NY: Seven Stories Press, 1998.

Goldman, Jonathon, "Introduction to Sound Healing" (online course). Accessed October 31, 2008. http://www.dailyom.com/cgi-bin/courses/displaycourselesson/cgi?pf=1&clid=163

Hawkins, David, M.D., Ph.D., *Power vs Force, The Hidden Determinants of Human Behavior*. Carlsbad, CA: Hay House, Inc., 1995.

Hay, Louise, *You Can Heal Your Life*. Carlsbad, CA: Hay House, Inc., 1984.

Hitt, Michael Olin, Ph.D., *A Fish Made of Water: An Oracle's Guide to the Spiritual Universe*. Vandalia, OH: Braided Way Media, LLC, 2011.

Newton, Michael, Ph.D., *Journey of Souls, Case Studies of Life Between Lives*. St. Paul, MN: Llewellyn Publications, 1994.

Newton, Michael, Ph.D., *Destiny of Souls, New Case Studies of Life Between Lives*. Woodbury, MN: Llewellyn Publications, 2000.

Oz, Mehmet, M.D., "Less Stress With Meditation: 3 Easy Steps." Written by Mao Shing Ni, L.Ac., D.O.M., PhD. Accessed October 20, 2012. http://www.doctoroz.com/blog/mao-shing-ni-lac-dom-phd/less-stress-meditation-3-easy-steps

Ruiz, Don Miguel, *The Four Agreements, A Toltec Wisdom Book*. San Rafael, CA: Amber-Allen Publishing, Inc., 1997.

Schwartz, Robert, *Your Soul's Plan: Discovering the Real Meaning of the Life You Planned Before You Were Born*. Berkeley, CA: Frog Books c/o North Atlantic Books, 2007.

Tipping, Colin C., *Radical Forgiveness, Making Room for the Miracle*. Marietta, GA: Global 13 Publications, Inc., 2002.

Tolle, Eckhart, *A New Earth, Awakening to Your Life's Purpose*. New York: The Penguin Group, 2006.

Virtue, Doreen, Ph.D., "About Doreen Virtue." Accessed October 20, 2012. http://www.angeltherapy.com

Virtue, Doreen, Ph.D., *Messages From Your Angels Cards*. Carlsbad, CA, 2002.

Vitale, Joe and Len, Ihaleakala Hew, Ph.D., *Zero Limits, The Secret Hawaiian System for Wealth, Health, Peace and More*. Hoboken, New Jersey: John Wiley & Sons, Inc., 2007.

Williamson, Marianne, *A Return to Love*. New York, NY: Harper Collins Publishers, Inc., 1992.

Zukav, Gary, *The Seat of the Soul*. New York, NY: Fireside, *1989*.

Made in the USA
Lexington, KY
04 June 2013